THE HAZARDOUS EARTH

THE COAST

Hazardous Interactions within the Coastal Environment

THE HAZARDOUS EARTH

THE COAST

Hazardous Interactions within the Coastal Environment

Timothy Kusky, Ph.D.

Facts On File

An imprint of Infobase Publishing

THE COAST: Hazardous Interactions within the Coastal Environment

Facts On File, Inc.
An imprint of Infobase Publishing
132 West 31st Street
New York NY 10001

Library of Congress Cataloging-in-Publication Data
Kusky, Timothy M.
  The coast: hazardous interactions within the coastal environment / Timothy Kusky.
      p. cm.—(The hazardous Earth)
  Includes bibliographical references and index.
  ISBN-13: 978-0-8160-6467-0
  ISBN-10: 0-8160-6467-9
  1. Coast changes. 2. Coastal zone management. I. Title.
  GB451.1.K87 2008
  551.45'7—dc22   2007042827

Facts On File books are available at special discounts when purchased in bulk quantities for businesses, associations, institutions, or sales promotions. Please call our Special Sales Department in New York at (212) 967-8800 or (800) 322-8755.

You can find Facts On File on the World Wide Web at http://www.factsonfile.com

Text design by Erika K. Arroyo
Illustrations by Melissa Ericksen and Richard Garratt
Photo research by Suzanne M. Tibor, Ph.D.

Printed in the United States of America

VB ML 10 9 8 7 6 5 4 3 2 1

This book is printed on acid-free paper and contains 30 percent postconsumer recycled content.

To Mom

■ ■ ■

Contents

Preface

Natural geologic hazards arise from the interaction of natural Earth processes and humans. Recent natural disasters such as the 2004 Indian Ocean tsunami that killed more than a quarter million people and earthquakes in Iran, Turkey, and Japan have shown how the motion of the Earth's tectonic plates can suddenly make apparently safe environments dangerous or even deadly. The slow sinking of the land surface along many seashores has made many of the world's coastal regions prone to damage by ocean storms, as shown disastrously by Hurricane Katrina in 2005. Other natural Earth hazards arise gradually, such as the migration of poisonous radon gas into people's homes. Knowledge of the Earth's natural hazards can lead one to live a safer life, providing guiding principles on where to build homes, where to travel, and what to do during natural hazard emergencies.

The eight-volume The Hazardous Earth set is intended to provide middle- and high-school readers with a readable yet comprehensive account of natural geologic hazards, the geologic processes that create the hazards to humans, and what can be done to minimize their effects. Titles in the set present clear descriptions of plate tectonics and associated hazards, including earthquakes, volcanic eruptions, landslides, and soil and mineral hazards, as well as hazards resulting from the interaction of the ocean, atmosphere, and land, such as tsunamis, hurricanes, floods, and drought. After providing the reader with an in-depth knowledge of naturally hazardous processes, each volume gives vivid accounts of historic disasters and events that have shaped human history and serve as reminders for future generations.

One volume covers the basic principles of plate tectonics and earthquake hazards, and another volume covers hazards associated with volcanoes. A third volume is about tsunamis and related wave phenomena, and another volume covers landslides, soil, and mineral hazards, which includes discussions of mass wasting processes, soils, and the dangers of the natural concentration of hazardous elements such as radon. A fifth volume covers hazards from climate change and drought changing the land surface, and how they affect human populations. This volume also discusses glacial environments and landforms, shifting climates, and desertification, all related to the planet's oscillations back and forth into ice ages and hothouses. Greater understanding is achieved by discussing environments on Earth that resemble icehouse (glaciers) and hothouse (desert) conditions. A sixth volume, entitled *The Coast*, includes discussion of hazards associated with hurricanes, coastal subsidence, and the impact of building along coastlines. A seventh volume, *Floods*, discusses river flooding and flood disasters, as well as many of the contemporary issues associated with the world's diminishing freshwater supply in the face of a growing population. This book also includes a chapter on sinkholes and phenomena related to water overuse. An eighth volume, *Asteroids and Meteorites*, presents information on impacts that have affected the Earth, their effects, and the chances that another impact may occur soon on Earth.

The Hazardous Earth set is intended overall to be a reference book set for middle school, high school, and undergraduate college students, teachers and professors, scientists, librarians, journalists, and anyone who may be looking for information about Earth processes that may be hazardous to humans. The set is well illustrated with photographs and other illustrations, including line art, graphs, and tables. Each volume stands alone and can also be used in sequence with other volumes of the set in a natural hazards or disasters curriculum.

Acknowledgments

Many people have helped me with different aspects of preparing this volume. I would especially like to thank my wife Carolyn, and my children Shoshana and Daniel for their patience during the long hours spent at my desk preparing this book. Without their understanding, this work would not have been possible. I also extend a special thanks to my parents for the time in their house on the eroding cliffs above the sea at Plymouth, Massachusetts. Frank K. Darmstadt, executive editor, reviewed and edited all text and figures, providing guidance and consistency throughout. I appreciate the excellent photo research provided by Suzie Tibor who is responsible for locating many of the excellent photographs in this volume. Many sections of the work draw from my own experiences doing scientific research in different parts of the world, and it is not possible to thank the hundreds of colleagues whose collaborations and work I have related in this book. For this volume, I especially thank my colleagues Drs. Li Guangxi, Wang Lu, and Li Sanzhong at the Ocean University of China, and Duncan Fitzgerald and Dee Caldwell of Boston University, who have helped me appreciate the coastal zone. Their contributions to the science that allowed the writing of this volume are greatly appreciated. I have tried to reference the most relevant works, or in some cases more recent sources that have more extensive reference lists. Any omissions are unintentional.

Introduction

Coastlines offer some of the best scenery and recreation areas of our country, yet they also rank among the most hazardous areas to live. The world's coastline extends for about 273,000 miles (440,000 km) and nearly half of the world's population lives within 60 miles (100 km) of the shoreline. The *coastal zone* is therefore perhaps the most critical zone for the world's economy, culture, and future survival. It is also one of the most dangerous environments, being the site of most of the world's deadliest disasters.

The coastal zone is difficult to define in terms of placing exact boundaries on where it begins and ends, but can be thought of as the region on the land that is influenced in some way by humidity, tides, winds, salinity, or biota from the sea. Coasts are of two main kinds: dominantly erosional systems and dominantly depositional systems. *Erosional coasts* include high-relief rocky shorelines, areas of coastal cliffs, and may include some depositional features such as *beaches. Depositional coastlines* are more varied, and include *deltas* at the mouths of rivers, *barrier island* systems, and reef and glaciated coasts.

Coastal regions are prone to strikes by *hurricanes,* are subject to beach and cliff erosion, and are constantly changing dynamic environments. These changes result from the constantly changing types of interactions among the ocean, atmosphere, land, and people. Coastlines naturally change with fluctuations in the seasons and longer-term *climate change,* yet when people develop coastal areas they try to stabilize the shoreline, creating a battle between natural and human

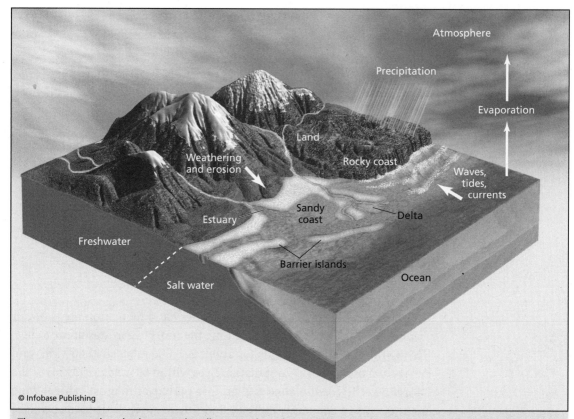

The ocean-atmosphere-land systems that all interact along the coast. The ocean brings waves, tides, and currents to the coast, and atmospheric systems often form over the ocean and bring moisture and wind to the land. The land provides freshwater to the coast, as well as the products of erosion and weathering. Beneath the surface in the ground water table there is a boundary between freshwater under the land and salt water under the sea. Diagram shows coastal environments including rocky and sandy shorelines, delta, estuary, and barrier islands.

forces. Despite these difficulties, coastal areas have become increasingly densely populated, even areas along fragile coastal islands. More than half of the population of the United States now lives within a one-day drive of the coast. Many of these areas are disasters waiting to happen, as one strike by a moderate-sized hurricane could totally devastate these regions, removing homes and potentially killing many people. Hurricane Katrina's devastation of New Orleans and the Gulf coast in 2005 is but a small taste of the devastating potential of coastal storms.

Coastal regions have distinctive landforms that represent a balance among forces from the ocean, land, and atmosphere. The plate tectonic setting largely determines the topographic style of the shoreline. Shores constructed along *passive continental margins,* located far from convergent boundaries, typically have wide *continental shelves* and sandy shorelines, with a few exceptions where ancient mountain belts such as the Appalachians in New England meet the shoreline. Many passive margin beaches in the Arctic and sub-Arctic regions are also rocky, as processes related to glaciation and uplift of the crust after the weight of the glaciers has been removed causes rocks to be exposed.

In contrast, most shorelines located along active or *convergent plate boundaries,* such as the west coast of the United States tend to be dominantly rocky, with many coastal bluffs. Shorelines along volcanic islands also tend to be rocky, since they are frequently replenished with new lava flows, and are prone to collapse, forming large escarpments.

The *biosphere,* or collection of organisms along a coast, also plays a significant role in shaping the shoreline. In tropical and subtropical regions, many shorelines are marked by dense mangrove forests and offshore coral reefs. These natural *ecosystems* are dynamic systems that respond rapidly to coastal changes, and also serve to protect interior areas from coastal hazards such as *storm surges* and *tsunamis.* Many areas with coastal mangroves and reefs have suffered great losses as a side effect of rapid coastal development. This destruction of coastal mangroves had disastrous consequences in the December 2004 Indian Ocean tsunami, when areas with dense mangroves were well-protected, but areas that had cleared mangrove forests saw much greater destruction.

Oceanic processes involving *tides,* coastal currents, and *rip currents* present many hazards to coastal residents. In some places the tidal range is several tens of feet, and great tidal bores move into bays and estuaries, potentially trapping the unsuspecting visitor. Tidal currents and bores can be quite strong, especially near coastal inlets, and in places where the water from incoming waves is channeled back out to deep water. Every year many swimmers and coastal vacationers are swept out to sea on clear days by hidden coastal currents.

Storms, especially late summer hurricanes and winter nor'easters, are capable of inflicting considerable damage to the shoreline. These storms are often preceded by a storm surge that may be tens of feet tall, and waves on top of the storm surge bring energy into shoreline environment at this new level, inflicting great damage. The storms also have high winds and heavy rainfall, and the combination of the battering from the sea and air leads to extremely rapid beach erosion during storms. The winds and rains can destroy beachfront homes, then the coastal erosion can remove the very beach on which these homes were built.

All beaches of the world have a risk of being hit by a tsunami, although the risk is greatest around the tectonically active Pacific Ocean. Local or distant *earthquakes, landslides,* or volcanic eruptions can displace large amounts of ocean water, forming a deepwater wave that moves at hundreds of miles per hour across ocean basins, and may rise unexpectedly on distant shorelines with run-up heights of several, tens, or occasionally hundreds of feet. Although tsunamis are rare, they pose a major risk to coastal environments.

Coastal regions are prone to changes at several different geologic timescales. Sea level is presently gradually rising at 1–4 feet (.3–1.2m) per century. Sea level rises and falls by hundreds of feet over periods of millions of years, forcing the position of the coastline to move inland and seaward by many tens of miles over long time periods. Most people do not think that changes over these time frames will affect their lives, but a *sea-level rise* of even a foot or two, which is possible over periods of tens of years, can cause extensive flooding, increased severity of storms, and landward retreat of the shoreline. Many current studies suggest that the rate of sea-level rise is increasing, and melting of the

Storm surge with waves crashing into buildings along the Malecon coastal highway in Havana, Cuba, October 24, 2005, after Hurricane Wilma. The ocean spread up to four blocks inland, flooding streets and buildings in up to three feet (1 m) of water. *(AP/ Eduardo Verdugo)*

polar ice caps could suddenly raise sea levels by many tens of feet, causing some of the most dramatic and costly environmental changes to the planet the human race has ever experienced.

Most changes to coastal areas are noticeable on shorter timescales, and may occur in single disastrous events. A large winter storm or summer hurricane can remove tens of feet (many meters) from coastal cliffs, can cause new channels to open up in barrier beach complexes, can cause extensive flooding and removal of buildings with strong tidal and storm surges, and can remove the vegetation from coastal areas. Damage, loss of property, and loss of life have risen dramatically along United States coastlines during each of the past few decades, as more and more of the population moves to coastal areas that are prone to hurricanes and storm damage. Many long-range climate forecasts predict that hurricanes will become more severe and more frequent over the next few decades, so these hazards will only grow more severe, and more planning is needed to mitigate the effects of storm damage.

Other hazards along coastlines are associated with changes on intermediate timescales—the slow but steady passage of coastal currents along a shoreline moves tons of sand daily along the coast, removing headlands and depositing the sand as bars and in harbors, both natural and human-made. Cliffs gradually collapse and the shoreline gradually retreats. Waves constantly pound the coast, eroding cliffs and seawalls, and carrying the sand and rock particles along the coast or out to sea.

The first chapter of *The Coast* describes characteristic landforms and environments found in the coastal zone, and follows with a chapter on the processes that form these landforms. Coastal hazards are also discussed in chapter 2, with examples of cliff erosion from wave and storm action, hazards associated with powerful tides, and the consequences of longshore sediment transport and people's futile attempts to control this process. Chapter 3 discusses the naturally changing shoreline, emphasizing that sea levels are constantly changing, now going through a period of sea-level rise. This causes the shoreline environment to move landward, which has important implications for residents of coastal areas. The coast is also sinking or subsiding in many places, from both natural and human-induced causes, with significant consequences as described in chapter 4.

Chapter 4 discusses some of the worst coastal disasters that have occurred in the period of 1900–2007, most of these being the effects of hurricanes on densely populated coastal areas. The chapter ends with a section on reducing the risks of coastal hazards, and how to plan for rising sea levels, increased storms, and larger populations. Issues of

Several houses destroyed by Hurricane Katrina, Ninth Ward, New Orleans, two years after the storm. *(Marc Pagani Photography, 2007, used under license from Shutterstock, Inc.)*

personal safety as well as community planning for these changing times are discussed.

Chapter 5 is about the nation's city that has the greatest risk and worst history of coastal disasters. New Orleans has been struck and virtually destroyed by hurricanes seven times since it was founded, the most recent and memorable time in 2005 with Hurricanes Katrina and Rita. The recurrence of disaster in New Orleans highlights human nature that, after a few years go by, the threat seems less. Disasters that repeat only once or twice a generation, or once every several generations, have historically claimed the most lives. Society needs to look at history rather than personal recollection to evaluate the safety and risks of rebuilding in an area that has suffered a major catastrophe. The geologic and natural history of New Orleans and why it is so at risk are discussed in this chapter. The chapter ends with a frank discussion of whether or not the city should keep on trying to rebuild in the same location, or if it is time to move to higher ground. A final chapter summarizes the book.

1

Characteristic Landforms and Environments of the Coastal Zone

The coastal zone to many people is the area between the highest point that tides influence the land, to the point at which the first breakers form offshore. The area of interaction of the land, sea, and atmosphere is actually much larger, and includes much of the continental shelf where long wavelength storm waves rustle the bottom, and extends inland to areas where onshore winds blow sand, humid air, increased salinity, and biota. In some cases the coastal zone may be considered to extend far into continental interior when coastal storms and hurricanes bring ocean energy far from the shoreline. Many subenvironments are characteristic of the coastal zone, including deltas, *reefs*, beaches, bays, *estuaries, tidal flats,* and wetlands, *lagoons,* barrier islands, and coastal cliffs. In this chapter, each of these subenvironments of the coastal zone is described. In the following chapter, processes that influence and change these different environments are discussed.

Coastal Environments

BEACH AND NEARSHORE ENVIRONMENT

Beaches are accumulations of sediment exposed to wave action along a coastline. The beach extends from the limit of the low-tide line, to the point inland where the vegetation and landforms change to that typical of the surrounding region. This may be a forest, a cliff, *dune,* or lagoon. Many beaches merge imperceptibly with grasslands and forests, whereas others end abruptly at cliffs or other permanent features

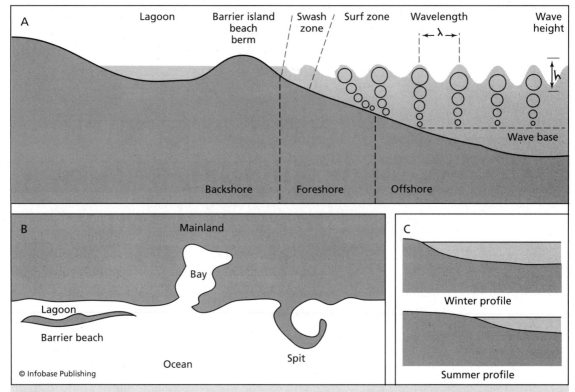

(A) Beach profile showing the major elements from the backshore to offshore; (B) different types of coastal environments, including barrier beaches, bays, and spits; (C) typical beach profiles in summer and winter showing how large winter storms erode the beach and smaller summer waves rebuild the beach.

including artificial seawalls that have been built in many places in the past century. Beaches may occupy bays between headlands, they may form elongate strips attached (or detached, in the cases of barrier islands) to the mainland, or they may form *spits* that project out into the water. To understand beaches, it is necessary to also consider the nearshore environment, the area extending from the low-tide line out across the surf zone. The nearshore environment may include sandbars, typically separated by troughs. The width of nearshore environments is variable, depending on the slope of the seafloor, wave dynamics, and availability of sediment. Most nearshore environments include an inner sandbar located about 100–165 feet (30–50 m) offshore, and another bar about twice as far offshore. The inner bar is often cut by channels known as rip channels that allow water that piles up between the bar and beach to escape back to sea, often generating dangerous rip-currents that can drag unsuspecting swimmers rapidly out to sea.

Most sandy beaches develop typical profiles that change through the seasons, and include several zones. These are the *ridge and runnel, foreshore, backshore,* and *storm ridge.* The ridge and runnel is the most seaward part of the beach, characterized by a small sandbar called a ridge, and a flat-bottom trough called the runnel, and is typically less than 30 feet (10 m) wide. The runnel is covered by water at high tide, and has many small sand ripples that are extensively burrowed into by worms, crabs, and other beach life.

The foreshore, or beachface, is a flat, seaward-sloping surface that grades seaward into the ridge and runnel, or the intertidal zone if the ridge and runnel are not present. A narrow zone of gravel or broken shells may be present at the small slope-break between the foreshore and the ridge and runnel. The foreshore contains the swash and back-wash zone, where waves move sand diagonally up the beachface parallel to the wave incidence direction, and gravity pulls the water and sand directly down the beachface parallel to the slope. This diagonal, then beach-perpendicular motion produces a net transport of sand and water along the beach, known as *longshore drift* and longshore currents.

The backshore extends from a small ridge and change in slope at the top of the foreshore known as a berm, to the next feature (dune, seawall, forest, lagoon) toward the land. This area is generally flat or gently landward sloping. The backshore area is generally dry and above the high water mark except during large storms, so the backshore area is mainly affected and shaped by wind. Some backshore areas are characterized by multiple berms, and others have none. On gravel beaches, found in high-energy environments, the backshore area may be replaced by a storm ridge marked by a several to 10-foot (3-m) high ridge of gravel. These ridges form because incoming waves have the velocity to move gravel up the beachface, but because this gravel is porous, the water sinks into the gravel before it can drag the gravel back down the beachface, resulting in their accumulation in a large ridge.

Beaches are highly variable in the width and heights of these various zones. Some beaches are steep while others are flat. Beaches that have flat slopes are said to be dissipative in that they take the energy from waves and gradually dissipate it across the intertidal zone. These types of beaches often have multiple sand bars in the nearshore environment. Reflective beaches are those with steep gradients, and these tend to take much of the wave energy and reflect it back to sea. Reflective beaches do not generally have nearshore bars, and are erosive in character.

Dissipative beaches tend to be depositional, as they are actively accreting sediment.

The shape of a beach is largely controlled by the nature of the waves, tides, currents, and to a lesser extent, wind. Waves move the sediment onshore, which is then transported along the beachface by the longshore currents, and perhaps blown to the backshore by wind. Tides serve to change the areas to which waves direct their energy vertically up and down, bringing the sediment alternatively to different sections of the beach. Out of all these processes, the currents produced by the waves on the beach are the most important. These currents include longshore currents, rip currents, onshore-offshore currents produced in the swash zone, and combined currents.

Beachface showing swash and backwash zone, with good sediment sorting on an Orkney Island beach, Scotland *(Alamy)*

Beaches are very dynamic environments and are always changing, being eroded and redeposited constantly from day to day and from season to season. Beaches are typically eroded to thin strips known as *storm beaches* by strong winter storms, and built up considerably during summer, when storms tend to be less intense. The wide summer beaches are known as *accretionary beaches*. The processes controlling this seasonal change are related to the relative amounts of energy in summer and winter storms—summer storms (except for hurricanes) tend to have less energy than winter storms, so they have waves with relatively short wavelengths and heights. These waves gradually push the offshore and nearshore sands up to the beachface, building the beach throughout the summer. In contrast, winter storms have more energy with longer wavelength, higher amplitude waves. These large waves break on the beach, erode the beachface and carry the sand seaward, depositing it in the nearshore and offshore environments. In some cases, especially along the rocky Pacific coasts, storms may remove all the sand from beaches, leaving only a rocky bedrock bench behind until the small summer waves can restore the beach. Storm beaches, however, tend to be temporary conditions as the wave energy decreases right after the storms, and even between winter storms, the beach may tend to rebuild itself to a wider configuration.

BARRIER ISLANDS

Barrier islands are narrow linear mobile strips of sand that are up to about 30–50 feet (10–15 m) above sea level, and typically form chains located a few to tens of miles offshore along many passive margins. They are separated from the mainland by the backbarrier region, which is typically occupied by lagoons, shallow bays, estuaries, or marshes. Barriers are built by vertical accumulation of sand from waves and wind action. Barrier islands are so-named because they represent a natural protection of the shoreline from the forces of waves, tsunamis, tides, and currents from the main ocean. However, many barrier islands have become heavily developed as they offer beautiful beaches and resort-type living. The development of barrier islands represents one

Space image taken from *Apollo 9* showing the barrier islands of the Outer Banks of Cape Hatteras, North Carolina, forming a thin line of mobile sand along the hurricane-prone coast. *(Science Source/Photo Researchers)*

of the most hazardous trends in coastal zones, since barriers are simply mobile strips of sand that move in response to changing sea levels, storms, coastal currents, and tides. Storms are capable of moving the entire sandy substrate out from underneath tall buildings.

The size of barrier islands ranges from narrow and discontinuous strips of sand that may be only a few hundred feet wide, to large islands that extend many miles across and also in length. The width and length is determined by the amount of sediment available as well as a balance between wave and tidal energy. Most barriers are built of sand—left over from glaciations (as in New England), eroded from coastal cliffs, or deposited by rivers along delta systems. Barrier island systems need to be discontinuous, to allow water from tidal changes to escape back to sea along systems of tidal inlets.

Subenvironments of barriers are broadly similar to those of beaches, and include the beach, barrier interior, and the landward interior. The beachface of a barrier is the most dynamic part of the island, absorbing energy from waves and tides, and responding much as beaches on

SHOULD PEOPLE LIVE ON BARRIER ISLANDS?

Some of America's favorite vacation and resort-living communities are located on barrier islands along the coast. People have flocked to places like Atlantic City, New Jersey; Ocean City, Maryland; Virginia Beach; Cape Hatteras, North Carolina; Myrtle Beach, South Carolina; Miami Beach and St. Petersburg in Florida; and Galveston, Texas. Some of these places have been preserved as National Seashores such as parts of the Outer Banks of North Carolina, but many others have been intensively developed. Rows of high-rise luxury apartments and condominiums line the beachfront along many of these resort communities, and people enjoy the sunny weather, waves, and sea breeze at the coast. More than half of America's population now lives within 60 miles (100 km) of the coast, showing that people have a natural tendency to appreciate the coastal environment. There is much to be said for living along the coast, yet there are also many risks and hazards that need to be accounted for as the coast continues to be developed.

On short timescales, coastal communities, especially those on low-lying barrier islands with limited access routes, have to be ready to respond to coastal hazards. The ocean is the breeding ground for the largest storm systems on the planet, including hurricanes, extratropical lows, and other systems. These storms bring enormous amounts of energy in the form of waves and wind to the shoreline, and can cause many years worth of average erosion in a single storm. Barrier islands are narrow strips of sand that are only slightly above sea level and are easily submerged by storm surges and large storm waves on top of the storm surge. The worst natural disasters in United States history include coastal storms inundating barrier islands, including the 1900 Galveston Island hurricane that killed about 10,000 people. Barrier islands are naturally mobile, with sand along the beachface moving up to half a mile (1 km) a day in longshore drift. Hurricanes have historically removed entire rows of houses and remobilized the coastal strip returning it to beach. That is why some barrier islands have the mainland do. The backside of the beach on many barrier islands is marked by a long frontal or *foredune ridge,* followed landward by secondary dunes. Barrier islands that have grown landward with time may be marked by a series of linear ridges that mark the former positions of the shoreline and foredune ridges, separated by low areas called *swales.* The landward margins of many barriers merge gradually into mud flats, salt marshes, or may open into lagoons, bays, or tidal creeks.

About 15 percent of the world's coastlines have barrier islands offshore, with most located along passive margin continental shelves, which have shallow slopes and a large supply of sediment available to build the barriers. In the United States, the eastern seaboard and the Gulf of Mexico exhibit the greatest development of barrier island systems. It seems that areas with low tidal ranges in low to middle climate zones have the most extensively developed barrier systems.

Barrier systems are of several types. *Barrier spits* are attached to the mainland at one end and terminate in a bay or the open ocean on the other end. They are most common along active tectonic coasts, although

a 3rd Street located along the coast—1st and 2nd have washed into the sea. Storms have opened new tidal inlets where only homes and streets were before, and closed others that were used for transportation to and from the mainland. A barrier island is also the most prone environment to other ocean hazards, including tsunamis, which occasionally wash up on most beaches of the world, including the Atlantic and Gulf of Mexico coasts of the United States.

Perhaps the most significant threat to barrier island development is the slow but inexorable rise of sea level. For every foot that sea level rises, most barrier island beaches will move inland by at least 50 feet (15 m). This is because when sea level rises, barrier islands try to maintain their equilibrium profile, and move each beach element landward along the relatively flat coastal plain. Over time, many barrier islands actually "roll over," where the sand from the outer beachface is transported over the berm to the backbeach area, then gets buried by new sand. As the sea level rises and the barrier moves landward, this sand eventually comes back out to the front of the barrier, completing a circuit as the barrier rolls over. While it is harmless to the sand grains to make many roll-over cycles like this, it is obviously not a stable environment to build on, no matter how large the structure. Building seawalls and other protective measures often takes the energy from incoming waves, and deflects it back out to the beach, causing the beach sands to be eroded, eventually undermining the wave protection structures. Eventually, the sea, and migrating sand barriers are sure to win. To many people, however, it is worth the risk to enjoy living on the coast. Other people question who should pay for taking this risk now that the risks are well understood. Should national tax-funded insurance pay for damage to homes built in such a risky zone, or should private owners pay through their own insurance? Should the costs be spread across the insurance market, or those who live in high-risk areas along the coast be made to pay an extra "high-risk" living tax?

Cape Cod, Massachusetts, is one of the better known examples of a spit formed along a passive continental margin. Some spits have ridges of sand that curve around the end of the spit that terminates in the sea, reflecting its growth. These are known as *recurved spits.* Sandy Hook, at the northern end of the New Jersey coast, is a recurved spit. Spits form as *longshore currents* carry sediment along a coastline, and the coastline makes a bend into a bay. In many cases the currents that carry the sand continue straight and carry the sediment offshore, depositing it in a spit that juts out from the mouth of the bay. Many other subcategories of spits are known, and are classified based on specific shape. Some, known as *tombolos,* may connect offshore islands with the mainland, whereas others have cuspate forms, or jut outward into the open water.

In some cases barriers grow completely across a bay and seal off the water inside the bay from the ocean. These types of barriers are known as *welded barriers,* and are most common along rocky coasts such as in New England and Alaska. Welded barriers seem to also form preferentially where tidal energy is low which prevents the tides from creating tidal channels that allow salty water to circulate into the bay. Some also form during onshore migration of barriers during times of sea-level rise, when the barrier sands get moved into progressively narrowing bays as they are forced to move inland. Since they are cut off from the ocean, bays behind welded barriers tend to be brackish or even filled with freshwater.

Barriers form by a variety of different mechanisms in different settings, but the most common mechanisms include the growth and accretion of spits that become breached during storms, growth as off-shore sand bars, and as submergence of former islands during times of sea-level rise. Barriers are constantly moving, and respond to storms, currents, waves, and sea-level rise by changing their position and shape. Barriers that are moving onshore are known as *retrograding barriers,* and move by a process of rolling over, where sand on the outer beach-face is moved to the backshore, then overrun by the next sand from the beachface. A continuation of this process leads the barrier to roll over itself as it migrates onshore. *Prograding barriers* are building themselves seaward, generally through a large sediment supply, whereas aggrading barriers are simply growing upward in place as sea levels rise.

opposite: Block diagrams of dune types including (A) barchan; (B) transverse; (C) barchanoid; (D) linear; (E) parabolic; and (F) star. The graph (triangular) shows different types of dunes produced by different combinations of wind strength, sand supply, and density of vegetation.

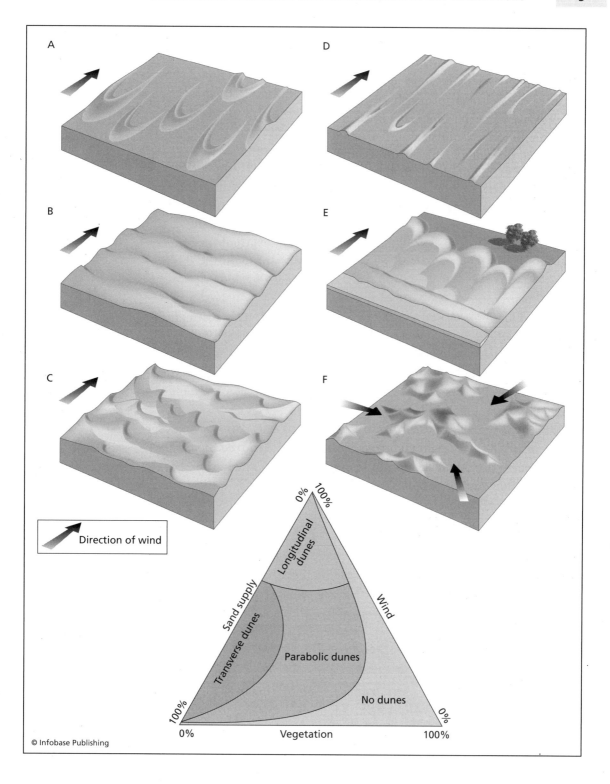

A

B

C

D

E

F

Direction of wind

0%
100%
0%

Longitudinal dunes

Sand supply

Wind

Transverse dunes

Parabolic dunes

No dunes

100%
0%

0%
Vegetation
100%

COASTAL DUNES

Many coastal areas have well-developed sand dunes in the backshore area, some of which reach heights of several tens or even hundreds of feet (tens of meters). The presence or absence of dunes, and their shape and height is mostly controlled by the amount of sediment supply available, although the wind strength and type and distribution of vegetation also play significant roles. Dunes represent fragile ecosystems that can easily be changed by disturbing the vegetation or beach dynamics, yet their importance is paramount to protecting inland areas from storm waves and surges, tsunamis, and other hazards from the ocean.

Most coastal dunes are of the linear type, and are called foredunes, forming elongate ridges parallel to the beach just landward of the foreshore. In some cases, numerous foredunes are present, with the ones closest to land being the oldest and the younger ones forming progressively seaward of these older dunes.

Sand dunes in the backbeach area by the windblown accumulation of sand derived from the foreshore area. The sands may grow far into the backshore environment, in some cases extending miles inland if not obstructed by vegetation, cliffs, or constructions such as buildings or seawalls. Vegetation is extremely effective at stabilizing mobile sand, and many examples of sand being trapped by plants are visible on beaches of the world.

Dunes are built by the slow accumulation of sand moved by wind, but may be rapidly eroded by storm surges, and wave attack when the

Coastal dunes developed in the backbeach area of the Persian Gulf, United Arab Emirates. Note the sand ripples on the dunes. *(T. Kusky)*

sea surface is elevated on storm surges. A single storm can remove years of dune growth in a few hours, transporting the dune sand offshore or along shore. Likewise, tsunamis can remove entire dune fields in a single devastating event, as seen in many places during the Indian Ocean tsunami of December 2004. Rising sea levels are posing a huge threat to many existing coastal dune fields, since a rise in sea level of 1 foot on flat terrain can be equated with a 100-foot (30-m) landward migration of the shoreline, and the removal of the dune field from one location to an area further inland, or to its complete elimination.

COASTAL LAGOONS

Lagoons are a special and rather rare class of restricted coastal bays that are separated from the ocean by an efficient barrier that blocks any tidal influx, and that do not have significant freshwater influx from the mainland. Water enters lagoons mainly from rainfall, and occasional storm wash-over. Evaporation from the lagoon causes the water to have elevated salinity, and distinctive environments and biota.

Most lagoons are elongate parallel to the coast and separated from the ocean by a barrier island, or in some cases by a reef. They are most common in dry or near-desert climates, since freshwater runoff needs to be very limited to maintain lagoon conditions. Lagoons are therefore common along coasts including the Persian Gulf, North Africa, southeast Africa, Australia, Texas, Mexico, and southern Brazil.

Many lagoons show large seasonal changes in salinity, with nearly fresh conditions during rainy seasons, and extremely salty conditions as the waters evaporate and even dry up in the dry seasons. Normal marine and estuarine organisms cannot tolerate such large variations in salinity, so typically large numbers of a relatively few specialized species of organisms are found in lagoons. Some species of fish, such as the killifish, can regulate the salinity in their bodies to match that of the outside waters, so they are well suited for the lagoon environment. Certain species of gastropods (snails) are also very tolerant to variations in salinity, and are found in large quantities in some lagoons.

As the water in lagoons evaporates in summer months, it deposits chemical sediments known as evaporates and carbonates. These typically include a sequence of minerals from aragonite to calcite to gypsum to halite. Many ancient lagoon environments are recognized by the presence of this repeating sequence of evaporate and carbonate minerals in the rock record.

Lagoons are not significantly influenced by waves or tides, and are dominated by effects of the wind. Winds can induce circulation in lagoons, or even waves during windstorms. Small wind-tides in lagoons may transport more water to one side of the lagoon, and deposit fine-grained sediments on this one side as the waters retreat when the wind dies out. During large ocean storms, tidal surges may overtop the barrier to the lagoon, bringing a surge of seawater and sediment into the lagoon. During storms, and during the daily sea breeze cycle, sand from the beach and coastal dunes can be transported into lagoons. This can be a major contributor to sediment accumulation in some lagoons, and in some examples, sand dunes from the beach are moving landward into lagoons, migrating over lagoonal sediments and vegetation.

Sediments deposited in lagoons include layers of chemical sediments that precipitated from the water as it evaporated, leaving the elements initially dissolved in the water behind as sedimentary layers. These sediments are most commonly fine-grained clay-sized calcite and aragonite, and form a carbonate mud known as micrite. Many lagoons are covered by mucky micrite layers that have green slimy microorganisms known as cyanobacteria, or blue-green algae, growing along the edges of the lagoon in the mud, and forming matlike pads surrounding the central, water-filled part of the lagoon. Many times these mudflats and algal pads are dried out and cracked by the sun, forming thin flakes that can be blown around by the wind. Lagoons also have sediments such as sand grains carried by the wind, and the skeletal and other remains of any of the organisms that lived in the lagoon. Sand washed into lagoons from storms often forms small fan-shaped bodies known as wash-over fans that cover parts of the lagoon on its seaward side.

TIDAL INLETS

Tidal inlets are breaks in barrier island systems that allow water, nutrients, organisms, ships, and people easy access and exchange between the high-energy open ocean and the low-energy backbarrier environment consisting of bays, lagoons, tidal marshes, and creeks. Most tidal inlets are within barrier island systems, but others may separate barrier islands from rocky or glacial headlands. Tidal inlets are extremely important for navigation between sheltered ports on the backbarrier bays and the open ocean, thus they are the sites of many coastal modifications such as jetties, breakwaters, and dredged channels to keep the channels stable and open.

Strong tidal currents move water into and out of tidal inlets as the tides wax and wane, and also carry large amounts of sediment out of the channel that are brought in by waves and longshore transport. Never try to swim in a tidal inlet. As tides rise on the ocean side of tidal inlets, the water rises faster than inside the inlet, since the inlet is narrow and it takes a long time for the water to move into the restricted environment behind the barrier. The difference in elevation causes the water to flow into the inlet with a strong current, called a flood-tidal current. As the tide falls outside the inlet, the reverse happens—as the tide falls quickly on the outside of the barrier, the sea surface is higher inside the inlet and a strong current known as an ebb-tidal current then flows out of the inlet, returning the water to the ocean. Considering the amount of time that it takes for water to flow into and out of tidal inlets, it is apparent that times of high and low tide may be considerably different on either sides of barrier systems connected by tidal inlets.

The sides of tidal inlets are often marked by curved sand ridges of recurved spits, formed as waves are refracted into the barrier and push the sand into ridges. The strongest currents in tidal inlets are found

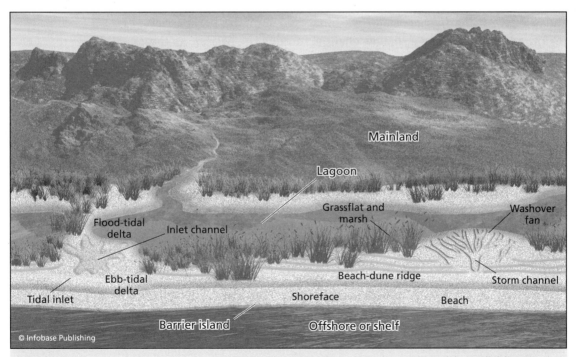

Map showing features of a barrier island, tidal inlet, lagoon coastal system. Note the positions of the small deltas on either side of the tidal inlet, the coastal marsh, and beach-dune ridges. *(Figure modified after Davis and Fitzgerald, 2004)*

where the inlet is the narrowest, a place with the deepest water called the inlet throat. Water rushes at high velocity into and out of this throat, carrying sand into and out of the backbarrier environment. Since the velocity of the water decreases after it passes through the throat, large lobes and sheets of sand are typically deposited as tidal deltas on both the inside and outside of tidal inlets. The delta deposited by the incoming (flood) tide on the inside or landward side of the inlet is known as a flood-tidal delta, whereas the delta deposited on the outside of the inlet by the ebb tide is known as an ebb-tidal delta.

Tidal inlets form by a variety of mechanisms. The most common is during the formation and evolution of barrier systems along coastal platforms on passive margins, where barrier islands formed as the glaciers retreated and sea levels rose onto the continental shelves in Holocene times. Sea levels slowed their rise about 5,000 years ago, and enhanced coastal erosion provided abundant sand to create the barrier island systems. The continued rising sea levels, plus diminished sediment supplies and the many modifications of the shoreline by people has led to increased erosion along much of the world's coastlines. With this trend, many barriers have been breached or cut-through during storms. Typically this happens when an incoming storm erodes the foredune ridge, and waves top the barrier island washing sand into the backbarrier region, and often making a shallow channel through the barrier. As the storm and elevated tides recede, the water in the backbarrier bay, lagoon, or tidal marsh is left high, then begins to escape rapidly through the new shallow opening, deepening it rapidly. If the tides can continue to keep this channel open, a new tidal inlet is established. Many tidal inlets along the Outer Banks barrier islands of North Carolina have formed in this way. Any homes or roads that were in the way, are gone.

Tidal inlets may also form by longshore currents building a spit across a bay or drowned river valley. As the spit grows across an open bay, the area that is open to the sea gradually becomes narrower, until it begins to host strong tidal currents, when it becomes deep, and reaches an equilibrium between the amount of sediment transported to the inlet by longshore drift, and the amount of sand moved out of the inlet by the tidal currents and waves.

INTERTIDAL FLATS

Many coastlines have flat areas within the tidal range that are sheltered from waves, dominated by mud, devoid of vegetation, and are accumulating sediment, known as intertidal (or just tidal) flats. The width of tidal flats depends on the tidal range and the shape and morphology of the coastline or bay they are located in. Some large bays with large tidal ranges, such as the Bay of Fundy in eastern Canada, are dominated by tidal flats. Tidal flats are typically flat areas cut by many channels, and dominated by mud and sandy sediment, and many may have layers of shell debris, and ecosystems of organisms specially adapted to this environment. They are alternately covered by water at high tide, and exposed to the atmosphere at low tide.

The sand, mud, and shell fragment layers that comprise most tidal flats are distributed in ways that reflect the distribution of energy in this environment. Sands are typically located near the base of the intertidal zone where energy from tides is the highest, and these sands gradually merge with and then give way to muds toward the upper parts of the zone, and away from the ocean. At any given location within the tidal flats, the sediments tend to be rather uniform in character, because of the similar conditions that persist and repeat at any given location.

Modern tidal flat environments are inhabited by a variety of organisms that are specially adapted to this harsh environment. These include specialized snails, worms, amphipods, oysters, mussels, and other bivalves. Many of these organisms survive by burrowing into the mud for protection, and in doing so, they destroy the fine-scale layering in the mud, in a process called bioturbation. The mud in many tidal flats is also inhabited by microscopic filamentous cyanobacteria (commonly called blue-green algae) that produce slimy mats that cover many mud surfaces, and serve to hold the mud particles together during the ebb and flow of the tides. These mucaceous mats also trap mud and other sediments, helping to build up the sedimentary accumulation in these environments.

Tidal flats often expose sediments in which the sedimentary particles are arranged in specific, peculiar, and repeating forms known as *sedimentary structures.* Familiar types of sedimentary structures include sedimentary layers; ripples, produced by currents moving the sedimentary particles as sets of small waves; mega-ripples, which are large ripples formed by unusually strong currents; mudcracks, produced by muddy sediments being dried by the sun and shrinking and cracking; and other structures produced by organisms. These latter structures include burrows from worms, bivalves, and other organisms; trails; and footprints.

Most tidal flats are cut by a network of tidal channels that may contain water even at low tides. These form a network of small to large channels, but are different from normal streams in that they carry water in different directions with the ebb and flood of the tides. As the tide rises into tidal flats strong currents that range up to several feet (1 m) per second bring the tidal wave through these channels, moving sediments throughout the flats. Tidal flats tend to slowly build themselves seaward, out from the bays or estuaries that they initially grow around. They may eventually fill in the bays and estuaries up to the sand dunes or berm in the backbeach area of the coastal barrier. Most tidal flats are not significantly affected by waves. However, exceptionally large flats such as the Wadden Sea area of the North Sea on Germany's coast are significantly affected by waves for several hours of each high tide stand.

COASTAL WETLANDS AND MARSHES

Many bays, estuaries, and coastal tidal flats are bordered inland by a vegetated intertidal area containing grasses or shrublike mangrove swamps. Mangroves do not tolerate freezing conditions, so are found only at low latitudes, whereas *salt marshes* are found at all latitudes. These coastal wetlands or salt marshes host a range of water salinities from salty and brackish to nearly fresh conditions. As estuaries age or mature, they tend to become progressively filled in first by tidal flats then by salt marshes or coastal wetlands. Thus, the degree to which estuaries are filled in can indicate the state of their maturity.

Salt marshes form on the upper part of the *intertidal zone* where organic, rich sediments are rarely disturbed by tides, providing a stable environment for grasses to take root. The low marsh area is defined as the part of the marsh that ranges from the beginning of vegetation to the least mean high tide. The high marsh extends from the mean high tide up to the limit of tidal influence. Different genera and species of grass form at different latitudes and on different continents, but in North America, high parts of salt marshes are dominated by Juncus grasses, also known as the needle- or black-rush, which can be five to six feet (1.5–1.8 m) tall, with sharp pointed ends. Low parts of salt marshes tend to be dominated by dense growths of knee-high Spartina grasses.

Salt marshes must grow upwards to keep up with rising sea levels. To do this they accumulate sediments derived from storm floods moving sediment inland from the beach environment, from river floods bringing in sediment from the mainland, and from the accumulation of organic material that grew and lived in the salt marshes. When plants in salt marshes are suddenly covered by sediment from storms or floods, they quickly recover by growing up through the new sediment, thereby allowing the marsh to survive and grow upward. Some salt marshes grow upward so efficiently that they raise themselves above tidal influence, and eventually become a freshwater woodland environment. However, with the increasing rate of sea-level rise predicted for the next century, many scientists are concerned that sea level will start to rise faster than marsh sedimentation can keep pace with. This problem is particularly exacerbated in places where the normal supply of river and flood sediments is cut off, for instance by levees along rivers. If this happens, many of the fragile and environmentally unique coastal marsh settings will disappear. Marshes are among the most productive of all environments on Earth, and serve as nurseries for many organisms, and are large producers of oxygen through photosynthesis. The disappearance of coastal marshes is already happening at an alarming rate in places such as the Mississippi River delta where coastal subsidence, loss of delta replenishment, together with sea-level rise leads to more than 0.39 inches (1 cm) of relative sea-level rise each year. Salt marshes are disappearing at an alarming rate along the Mississippi River delta, as discussed in chapter 3.

Many coastal marshes in low latitudes are covered with dense mangrove tidal forest ecosystems, also known as *mangals*. These have fresh to brackish water, and are under tidal influence. Mangrove stands have proven to be extremely effective protective barriers against invaders from the sea, including hostile navies, storm surges, and tsunamis. The destruction of many coastal mangrove forests in recent years has proven catastrophic to some regions, such as areas inundated by the 2004 Indian Ocean tsunamis that were once protected by mangroves. Many local governments removed the mangroves to facilitate development and shrimp farming, but when the tsunami hit, it swept far inland in areas without mangroves, and was effectively stopped in places where the mangroves still were undisturbed. There are many examples of where mangrove-dominated coasts have withstood direct hits from hurricanes and storm surges, and have protected the coastline to the extent that there was very little detectable change after the storm.

There are several dozen or more types of mangroves known, occurring on many coasts of North America, Africa, South America, India, Southeast Asia, and around the Pacific. Mangroves prefer protected low-energy coasts such as estuaries, lagoons, and backbarrier areas. Mangroves develop extensive root systems, and propagate by dropping seeds into the water, where they take root and spread. Mangrove stands have also been known to be uprooted by storms, float to another location, and take root in the new setting.

The extensive root network of mangrove stands slows many tidal currents and reduces wave energy by a factor of 10, forming lower-energy conditions inside the mangrove forest. These lower-energy conditions favor the deposition of sediment, enhancing seaward growth of the mangrove forest.

ESTUARIES

Estuaries are coastal embayments with a river flowing into one end and open to the sea at the other end; they are influenced by tides and waves from the sea, and also have significant freshwater influence from the land. Estuaries accumulate sediment from the river systems from the mainland as well as from the coast and tend therefore to fill in gradually over time. Each estuary is a unique environment that also preserves a range of water chemistry, reflecting a gradual mixing of the fresh river water from the land and salt water from the ocean. Salt water is denser than freshwater, however (having 3.5 percent dissolved salt), and tends in many cases to form a lens that underlies a freshwater cap across the surface of the estuary. The exact nature of the mixing depends on seasonal changes in freshwater influx, basin shape, depth, the wave energy, tidal range, and climate. Some estuaries preserve stratified water with salt water below and freshwater on top, whereas others show complex mixing between the different water types. The biota of estuaries are diverse, reflecting the large range in environments available for different species.

Different parts of estuaries are dominated by river and others by tidal processes. Rivers that enter large estuaries tend to form *bayhead deltas* that prograde into and may eventually fill the estuary. In other examples, such as Chesapeake Bay, many small rivers may enter the estuary and few have any significant delta since the river valleys in this system trap most of the stream sediment. Estuaries that are bordered seaward by barrier islands have much less tidal influence than those that have open mouths to the sea, although the tidal range and size and shape of the estuary also play large roles in determining the strength of tidal versus riverine processes. Estuaries that are tidal-dominated tend to lack barrier islands at their mouths, and exhibit funnel-shaped shorelines that amplify the tides by forcing the incoming tides into progressively more confined spaces. Estuaries that are tidal-dominated with strong tidal currents tend to have well mixed waters and sandy bottoms, whereas river-dominated estuaries often have stratified water columns and muddy bottoms. Most estuaries exhibit a range of different conditions in different parts—river conditions predominate at the head of the bay, tidal processes dominate at the mouth, and a mixed zone occurs in the middle. An extremely diverse biota inhabits estuaries, with organisms that prefer salty, high-energy conditions situated at the mouth of the estuary, and freshwater species found near the bayhead. Organisms that are tolerant of *brackish* conditions and can adapt to changing salinities and energy are typically found in between the zone of mixing.

DELTAS

Deltas are low, flat deposits of alluvium at the mouths of streams and rivers that form broad triangular- or irregular-shaped areas that extend into bays, oceans, or lakes. They are typically crossed by many distributaries from the main river, and may extend for a considerable distance underwater. Deltas are extremely sensitive coastal environments and are particularly susceptible to the effects of rising sea level and human activities. Since deltas are the sites of rich oil deposits, there is currently a sensitive interplay between meeting the world's energy needs by extracting oil from beneath the fragile delta environment, and adressing the environmental concerns about preserving the delta ecosystem.

The velocity and capacity of a stream to hold sediment suddenly drops when it enters the relatively still body of water such as a lake or the ocean. Thus, the stream dumps its sediment load here, and the resulting deposit is known as a delta. The term *delta* was first used for these deposits by Herodotus in the fifth century B.C.E. for the triangular-shaped alluvial deposits at the mouth of the Nile River. The stream first drops the coarsest material, then progressively finer material further out, forming a distinctive sedimentary deposit. In a study of several small deltas in ancient Lake Bonneville, Grover Karl Gilbert in 1890 recognized that the deposition of finer-grained material further away from the shoreline also resulted in a distinctive vertical sequence in delta deposits. The resulting foreset layer is thus graded from coarse nearshore to fine offshore. The bottomset layer consists of the finest material, deposited far out. As this material continues to build outward, the stream must extend its length, and form new deposits, known as topset layers, on top of all this. Topset beds may include a variety of subenvironments, both subaqueous and subaerial, formed as the delta progrades seaward.

Most of the world's large rivers such as the Mississippi, the Nile, and the Ganges, have built enormous deltas at their mouths, yet all of these are different in detail. Deltas may have various shapes and sizes or may even be completely removed, depending on the relative amounts of sediment deposited by the stream, the erosive power of waves and tides, the climate, and the tectonic stability of the coastal region. Most deltas are located along passive or trailing continental margins, and very few are found along convergent boundaries (exceptions include the Copper River in Alaska, and the Fraser River in British Columbia). This is largely because river systems on passive margins tend to be long and to drain huge areas composed of easily eroded soil, carrying large sediment loads. Rivers along active margins tend to be much shorter, and cut through bedrock, which is not eroded as easily, so yields smaller sediment loads. Additionally, convergent margins do not contain wide continental shelves that are needed for the delta to be deposited on, but instead, are marked by deep-sea trenches where sediments are rapidly deformed and buried.

Most deltas are quite young, having formed since the glaciers melted 18,000–10,000 years ago and sea levels rose onto the continental shelves. During the last glacial maximum when glaciers were abundant for much of the period from 2.5 million years ago until about 18,000 years ago, sea levels were about 395 feet (120 m) lower than at present. During the glacial maximum, most rivers eroded canyons across the continental shelves and carried their sedimentary load to the deep oceans. As the glaciers melted, sea level rose onto the broad continental shelves of many continents, where wide and thick delta sediments have space to accumulate. Nearly all of the active parts of deltas of the world are younger than 18,000 years, but many have older deeper parts that formed during older sea level high stands (some from interglacial periods) that have subsided deep below sea level. Since sea levels were initially rising very fast as the glaciers were undergoing rapid melting, the river mouths were moving so rapidly inland that deltas did not have time to form. The rate of sea-level rise slowed significantly around 6,000 years ago and most of the world's deltas began to grow significantly since that time. This history of sedimentation is reflected in the Mississippi River delta, which has components that are older

opposite: Three different types of deltas based on the relative strength of sediment input, tidal energy, and wave energy. The shapes of deltas characteristic of each are shown on the edges of the diagram, and names of other deltas of the world plotted in the space inside the diagram, in positions that reflect the relative strength for each delta. *(Figure modified from Galloway and Hobday, 1983)*

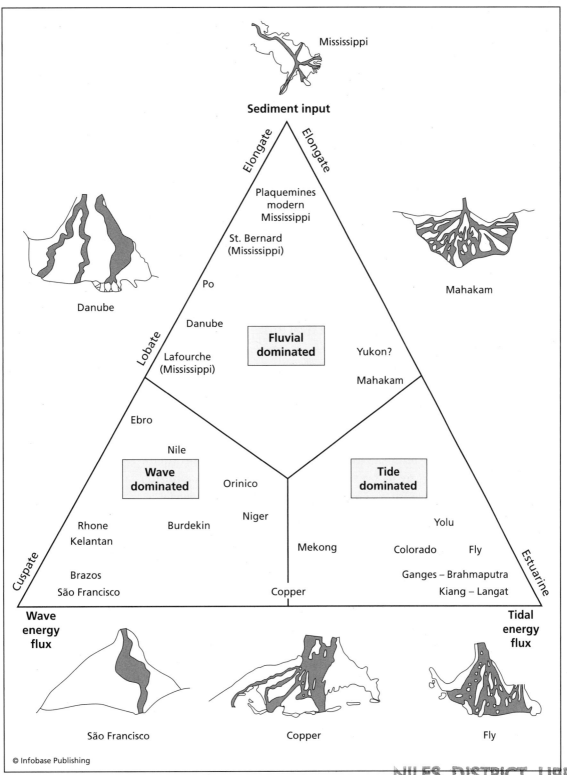

Mississippi

Sediment input

Elongate　Elongate

Plaquemines
modern
Mississippi

St. Bernard
(Mississippi)

Danube

Po

Lobate

Danube

Mahakam

Lafourche
(Mississippi)

**Fluvial
dominated**

Yukon?

Mahakam

Ebro

Nile

**Wave
dominated**

Orinico

**Tide
dominated**

Niger

Rhone
Kelantan

Burdekin

Yolu

Mekong

Colorado　Fly

Cuspate

Brazos

Ganges – Brahmaputra

São Francisco

Copper

Kiang – Langat

Estuarine

**Wave
energy
flux**

**Tidal
energy
flux**

São Francisco

Copper

Fly

than several million years, but the active lobes only began forming also about 6,000 years ago.

Deltas exhibit a range in conditions and environments from terrestrial- and river-dominated at their landward boundaries, to marine- and wave- and tide-dominated at their fronts. The mere presence of a delta along a coast indicates that the amount of sediment input by the river is greater than the amount of sediment that can be removed by the action of waves, tides, currents, wind, and submarine *slumping*. The distributaries and main channel of the rivers forming deltas typically move to find the shortest route to the sea, resulting in the shifting of the active locus of deposition on deltas. Inactive areas, which may form lobes or just parts of the delta, typically subside and are reworked by tidal currents and waves. The processes involved in the growth or seaward progradation of deltas results in the formation of many environments, including those influenced by subaerial, intertidal, and subaqueous processes, and include freshwater, brackish, and saltwater conditions. Most deltas can be divided into three main parts, the landward delta plain, the delta front, and the prodelta in the subtidal to deep continental shelf environment.

The *delta plain* is really a coastal extension of the river system. It is comprised of river and overbank sedimentary deposits, in a flat meandering stream type of setting. These environments are at or near (or in some cases below) sea level, and it is essential that the overbank regions receive repeated deposits of muds and silts during flood stages to continuously build up the land surface as the entire delta subsides below sea level by tectonic processes. Deltas deprived of this annual silt by the construction of levees gradually sink below sea level. However, if homes were built on delta flood plains without levees, they would gradually be buried in mud, as opposed to sinking below sea level behind the false protection of a levee. The stream channels are bordered by natural levee systems that may rise several feet (1–2 m) above the flood plain, these areas are often the only places above sea level during river flood stages. In many outer delta plains, the only places above sea level are the natural levees. During floods the levees sometimes break, creating a crevasse splay that allows water and muddy sediment to rapidly flow out of the channel and cover the overbank areas, including any homes or human infrastructure built in this sensitive area.

The delta front environment is located on the seaward edge of the delta, and is an extremely sensitive environment. It is strongly affected by waves, tides, changing sea level, and changes to the flux or amount of sediment delivered to the delta front. Many delta fronts have an off-shore sandbar known as a distributary mouth bar, or barrier island system, parallel to the coast along the delta front. Some deltas, such as the Mississippi are losing huge areas of delta front to subsidence below sea level, as combined effects of a decrease in sediment supply to the delta front, tectonic subsidence, sea-level rise, human activities such as oil drilling and building levees, and severe erosion from storms such as Hurricane Katrina.

Deltas have been classified various ways over time, including schemes based on their shapes, and on the processes involved in their construction. *High-constructive deltas* form where the fluvial transport dominates the energy balance on the delta. These deltas, dominated by riverine processes, are typically elongate, such as the modern delta at the mouth of the Mississippi, which has the shape of a birdsfoot, or they may be lobate in shape, such as the older Holocene lobes of the Mississippi that have now largely subsided below sea level.

High-destructive deltas form where the tidal and wave energy is high and much of the fluvial sediment gets reworked before it is finally deposited. In wave-dominated high-destructive deltas, sediment typically accumulates as arcuate barriers near the mouth of the river. Examples of wave-dominated deltas include the Nile and the Rhone deltas. In tide-dominated high-destructive deltas, tides rework the sediment into linear bars that radiate from the mouth of the river, with sands on the outer part of the delta sheltering a lower-energy area of mud and silt deposition inland from the segmented bars. Examples of tide-dominated deltas include the Ganges, and the Kikari and Fly River deltas in the Gulf of Papua, New Guinea. Other rivers drain into the sea in places where the tidal and wave current is so strong that these systems completely overwhelm the fluvial deposition, removing most of the delta. The Oronoco River in South America has had its sediment deposits transported southward along the South American coast, with no real delta formed at the mouth of the river.

Where a coarse sediment load of an alluvial fan dumps its load in a delta, the deposit is known as a fan-delta. Braid-deltas are formed when braided streams meet local base level and deposit their coarse-grained load.

Deltas create unique and diverse environments where fresh and saltwater ecosystems meet, and swamps, beaches, and shallow marine settings are highly varied. They contain some of the most productive ecological areas in the world. However, deltas also form some of the world's greatest hydrocarbon fields, as the muds and carbonates make good source rocks and the sands make excellent trap rocks. Thus, there is a delicate struggle between preserving natural ecosystems and using the planet's resources that must be maintained on the deltas of the world. Resting at sea level, delta environments are also the most susceptible to disaster from hurricanes and coastal storms.

Glacially carved fiord forming steep-sided rocky coast on the Kenai Peninsula of Alaska *(T. Kusky)*

GLACIATED COASTS

Glaciated and recently deglaciated coastlines offer a variety of environments that are significantly different from other coastal features so far discussed. Some coastlines, such as many in Antarctica, Greenland, and Alaska, have active glaciers that reach the sea, whereas other coasts, such as from New England northward into Canada, Scandinavia, and parts of the Far East, have recently been deglaciated (within the past 18,000 years).

The primary effects of glaciers on coastlines include the carving out of wide U-shaped glacial valleys and erosion of loose material overlying bedrock, the deposition of huge quantities of sediment especially near the terminus of glaciers, and lowering of global sea levels during periods of widespread glaciation. In addition, many coastal areas that had thick ice sheets on them were depressed by the weight of the glaciers, and have been slowly rebounding upwards since the weight of the glaciers was removed. This glacial rebound causes coastal features to move seaward, and causes former beaches and coastlines to be uplifted.

When glaciers move across the land surface, they can erode bedrock by a combination of grinding and abrasion, plucking material away from the bedrock; ice wedging where water gets in cracks expands as it freezes, and pushes pieces of bedrock away from its base. The material removed from the bedrock and overburden is then transported with the glacier to its end point, often at the coast, where it may be deposited as a pile of gravel, sand, and boulders known as a *glacial moraine.* Some glacial moraines are relatively small, and outline places where individual glaciers flowed out of valleys and ended at the sea. These form where the glaciers were relatively small and were confined to valleys. Other glacial moraines are huge, and mark places where continental ice sheets made

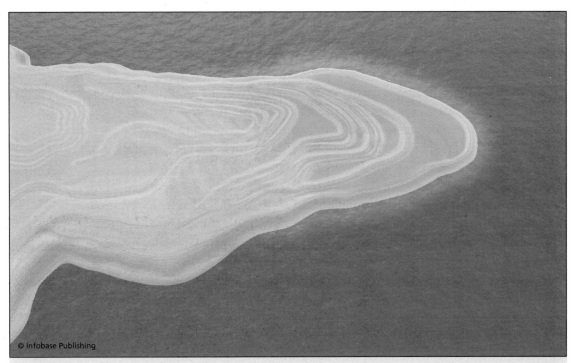

Aerial view of raised beaches caused by rapid isostatic rebound of the land since the last glaciation. View is of Arctic coast near Bathurst Inlet, Nunavut, Canada. *(Fletcher & Baylis/Photo Researchers Inc.)*

their farthest movement southward, depositing vast piles of sand and gravel at their terminus. On the eastern seaboard of the United States, New York's Long Island, and Massachusetts's Cape Cod, Martha's Vineyard, and Nantucket represent the complex terminal moraine from the Pleistocene ice sheets. In places like New England that were covered by large continental ice sheets, the glaciers tended to scour the surface to the bedrock, leaving behind irregular and rocky coasts characterized by promontories and embayments, islands, but only rare sandy beaches.

Depositional features on deglaciated coasts are varied. Glacial drift is a general term for all sediment deposited directly by glaciers, or by glacial meltwater in streams, lakes, and the sea. *Till* is glacial drift that was deposited directly by the ice. It is a nonsorted, random mixture of rock fragments. *Glacial marine drift* is sediment deposited on the seafloor from floating ice shelves or bergs, and may include many isolated pebbles or boulders that were initially trapped in glaciers on land, then floated in icebergs that calved off from tidewater glaciers. These rocks melted out while over open water, and fell into the sediment on the bottom of the sea. These isolated stones are called dropstones, and are often one of the hallmark signs of ancient glaciations in rock layers that geologists find in the rock record. Stratified drift is deposited by meltwater, and may include a range of sizes, deposited in different fluvial or lacustrine environments.

Terminal or end *moraines* are ridgelike accumulations of drift deposited at the farthest point of travel of a glacier's terminus. Terminal moraines may be found as depositional landforms at the bases of mountain or valley glaciers marking the locations of the farthest advance of that particular glacier, or may be more regional in extent, marking the farthest advance of a continental ice sheet. There are several different categories of terminal moraines, some related to the farthest advance during a particular glacial stage, and others referring to the farthest advance of a group of or all glacial stages in a region. Continental terminal moraines are typically succeeded poleward by a series of recessional moraines marking temporary stops in the glacial retreat or even short advances during the retreat. They may also mark the boundary between glacial outwash terrain toward the equator, and knob and kettle or hummocky terrain toward the pole from the moraine. The knob and kettle terrain is characterized by knobs of outwash gravels and sand separated by depressions filled with finer material. Many of these kettle holes were formed when large blocks of ice were left by the retreating glacier, and the ice blocks melted later leaving large pits where the ice once was. Kettle holes are typically filled with lakes and many regions characterized by many small lakes have a recessional kettle hole origin.

Glacial erratics are glacially deposited rock fragments with compositions different than underlying rocks. In many cases the erratics are composed of rock types that do not occur in the area they are resting in, but are only found hundreds or even thousands of miles away. Many glacial erratics in the northern part of the United States can be shown to have come from parts of Canada. Sediment deposited by streams washing out of glacial moraines is known as outwash, and is typically deposited by braided streams. Many of these form on broad plains known as outwash plains. When glaciers retreat, the load is diminished, and a series of outwash terraces may form.

Drumlins are teardrop-shaped accumulations of till that are up to about 150 feet (50 m) in height, and tend to occur in groups of many drumlins. These have a steep side that faces in the direction from which the glacier advanced, and a backside with a gentler slope. Drumlins are thought to form beneath ice sheets and record the direction of movement of the glacier. Drumlin coasts are found on the eastern side of

Nova Scotia, and in Massachusetts Bay. A final common depositional landform of glaciers found on many coasts are eskers, elongate ridges of sands and gravel that may extend many miles, but be only a few tens of feet (several m) wide. These represent the paths of meltwater streams that flowed inside and underneath the glaciers, depositing the sand and gravel in the stream bed, which got left behind as the glacier retreated.

Coastlines that were mountainous when the glaciers advanced had their valleys deepened by the glaciers carving out their floors and sides, creating fiords. *Fiords* are steep-sided glacial valleys that open to the sea. Southern Alaska has numerous fiords that have active tidewater glaciers in them, which are now experiencing a phase of rapid retreat. The Hudson River Valley and Palisades just north of New York City comprise a fiord formed in the Pleistocene, and many fiords are found in Scandinavia, New Zealand, Greenland, Chile, and Antarctica.

ROCKY COASTS

Rocky coastlines are most common along many convergent tectonic plate boundaries and on volcanic islands, but may also be found on recently deglaciated coasts and along some other uplifted coasts such as southern Africa and recently uplifted coasts such as along the Red Sea. Rocky coasts are the most common type of coastline in the world, comprising on the order of 75 percent of the world's coasts. The morphology of rocky coastlines is mainly determined by the type of rock, its internal structure, tectonic setting, as well as the physical, chemical, and biological processes operating on the coastline. Coastlines with mountains and steep slopes under the sea tend to have large waves, since little of the wave energy is dissipated by shallow water as the waves approach. These large waves erode the coast and also transport any sand that tends to accumulate offshore, so it is rare to find sandy beaches on steep rocky coastlines. Some tropical islands have exposures of jagged limestone along their coastlines. Much of this limestone formed as shallow water mud and reefs, and was exposed above sea level when sea levels fell during the Pleistocene.

The rates of geological processes and change along rocky coastlines is much slower than along sandy beaches, so it is often difficult to notice change over individual lifetimes. However, rocky coastlines are experiencing erosion over geological time periods, through a combination of waves, rain, ice-wedging during the freeze-thaw cycle, and chemical and biological processes. Waves that continuously pound on rocky coastlines are the most effective erosive agents, slowing the wearing down of the rock, and in some cases quarrying away large boulders. When waves carry sand and smaller rocks, these particles are thrown against the coastal rocks, causing significant abrasion and erosion. Abraded rock surfaces tend to be smooth, whereas those eroded by quarrying by waves are irregular.

In higher latitudes that are subject to the freeze-thaw cycle, water often gets trapped in cracks and joints in the rock, then freezes. Since water expands by 9 percent when it freezes, this creates large stresses on the rock around the crack, which are often enough to expand the crack and eventually contribute to causing blocks of rock to separate from the main rocky coast, and become a boulder.

Biological processes also contribute to the erosion of rocks along rocky coasts. Microscopic blue-green algae burrow into limestone, using the calcium carbonate ($CaCO_3$) as a food, and causing the limestone to be more easily weathered away, a fraction of an inch (mm) at a time. Other organisms, such as sea urchins, abalone, chitons, and other invertebrates bore into rocky substrate, slowly eroding the coast. Rocks along the coast are also subject to *chemical weathering,* just as other

Rocky shoreline, northern California *(T. Kusky)*

rocks in other environments are. Limestones may be dissolved by acid rain, and feldspars in granites and other rocks may be converted into soft, easily eroded clay by hydrolysis.

The relative strength of these processes is determined by several factors, including rock type, climate, wave energy, rock structure, tidal range, and sea level. Soft rocks such as sandstones are easily eroded, whereas granites weather much more slowly, and typically form headlands along rocky coasts. Rocks that are highly fractured tend to break and eroded faster, especially in climates with a significant freeze-thaw cycle. In humid wet climates chemical erosion may be more important than the freeze-thaw cycle. Wave height and energy is important, and exert their greatest erosive power at just above the mean high water level, and are very effective at slowly removing rocks, seawalls, and other structures particularly in places of times that sandy beaches are absent. Sandy beaches absorb wave energy, so when beaches are absent the waves are much more erosive. Areas with small tidal ranges tend to keep the wave energy focused on a small area, whereas areas with large tidal ranges tend to always change the area being attacked by waves. Thus, tides, and relative sea level also influence the effectiveness of waves in eroding the coast.

Many rocky coasts are bordered by steep cliffs, many of which are experiencing active erosion. The erosion is a function of waves under-cutting the base of the cliffs and oversteepening the slopes, which then collapse forming a pile of boulders that then are broken down by wave action. On volcanic islands such as Hawaii and Cape Verde, some large, amphitheater-shaped cliffs were formed by giant landslides when large sections of these islands slumped into the adjacent ocean, creating the cliffs and generating tsunamis. In contrast, cliffs of unconsolidated gravel and sand attempt to recover to the *angle of repose* by rain water erosion or slumping from the top of the cliff. This erosion can be dramatic, with many tens of feet removed during single storms. The material that is eroded from the cliffs replenishes the beaches, and without the erosion the beaches would not exist. Coarser material is left behind as it cannot be transported by the waves or tidal currents, and these typically form a rocky beach with a relatively flat platform known as a wave-cut terrace.

Some rocky shorelines are marked by relatively flat bedrock platforms known as *benches,* ranging from a few tens of feet (m) to thousands of feet (1 km) wide, typically followed inland by cliffs. These benches may be horizontal, gently seaward dipping, or inclined as much as 30 degrees toward the sea. Benches are formed by wave abrasion and quarrying of material away from cliffs, and develop along with cliff retreat from the shoreline. The waves must have enough energy to remove the material that falls from the cliffs, and the waves abrade the surface during high tides. Benches developed on flat-lying sedimentary rocks tend to be flat, whereas those developed on other types of rocks may be more rugged. An unusual type of chemical weathering may also play a role in the formation of wave-cut benches. The alternate wetting and drying leaves sea salts behind that promote weathering of the rock, making it easier for the waves to remove the material.

Along many coastlines wave-cut benches or platforms may be found at several different levels high above sea level. These *marine terraces* generally form where tectonic forces are uplifting the coastline, such as along some convergent margins, and can be used to estimate the rates of uplift of the land if the ages of the various marine terraces can be determined.

A variety of other unusual erosional landforms are found along rocky shorelines, particularly where cliffs are retreating. *Sea stacks* are isolated columns of rock left by retreating cliffs, with the most famous being the Twelve Apostles along the southern coast of Australia. Arches are sometimes preserved in areas of seastacks that have developed in horizontally layered sedimentary rocks, where waves erode tunnels through headlands.

REEF SYSTEMS

Reefs are wave-resistant, framework-supported carbonate or organic mounds generally built by carbonate secreting organisms; in some usages the term *reef* may be used for any shallow ridge of rock lying near the surface of the water. Reefs contain a plethora of organisms that together build a wave-resistant structure to just below the low tide level in the ocean waters, and provide shelter for fish and other organisms. The spaces between the framework are typically filled by skeletal debris, which together with the framework become cemented together to form a wave-resistant feature that shelters the shelf from high-energy waves. Reef organisms (at present consisting mainly of zooxanthellae, such as dinoflagellate algae) can only survive in the photic zone, so reef growth is restricted to the upper 328 feet (100 m) of the seawater.

Reefs are built by a wide variety of organisms, today including red algae, mollusks, sponges, and cnidarians (including corals). The colonial Scleractinia corals are presently the principal reef builders, producing a calcareous external skeleton characterized by radial partitions known as septa. Inside the skeleton are soft-bodied animals called polyps, containing symbiotic algae that are essential for the life cycle of the coral, and the building of the reef structure. The polyps contain calcium bicarbonate that is broken down into calcium carbonate, carbon dioxide, and water. The calcium carbonate is secreted to the reef building its structure, whereas the algae photosynthesize the carbon dioxide, producing food for the polyps.

There are several different types of reefs, classified by their morphology and relationship to nearby landmasses. Fringing reefs grow along and fringe the coast of a landmass, and are often discontinuous. They typically have a steep outer slope, an algal ridge crest, and a flat, sand-filled channel between the reef and the main shoreline. Barrier reefs form at greater distances from the shore than fringing reefs, and are generally broader and more continuous than fringing reefs. They are among the largest biological structures on the planet—for instance, the Great Barrier Reef of Australia is 1,430 miles (2,300 km) long. A wide, deep lagoon typically separates barrier reefs from the mainland. All these reefs show a zonation from a high-energy side on the outside or windward side of the reef, and typically grows fast, and has a smooth outer boundary. In contrast, the opposite side of the reef receives little wave energy, and may be irregular, poorly developed, or merge into a lagoon. Many reefs also show a vertical zonation in the types of organisms present, from deep water, to shallow levels near the sea surface.

Atolls or atoll reefs form circular, elliptical, or semicircular shaped islands made of coral reefs that rise from deep water, atolls surround central lagoons, typically with no internal landmass. Some atolls do have small central islands, and these, as well as parts of the outer circular reef, are in some cases covered by forests. Most atolls range in diameter from half a mile to over 80 miles (1–130 km) and are most common in the western and central Pacific Ocean basin, and in the Indian Ocean. The outer margin of the semicircular reef on atolls is the most active site of coral growth, since it receives the most nutrients from upwelling waters on the margin of the atoll. On many atolls, coral growth on the outer margin is so intense that the corals form an overhanging ledge from which many blocks of coral break off during storms, forming a huge *talus* slope at the base of the atoll. Volcanic rocks, some of which lie more than half a mile (1 km) below current sea level, underlay atolls. Since corals can only grow in very shallow water less than 65 feet (20 m) deep, the volcanic islands must have formed near sea level, grown coral, and subsided with time, with the corals growing at the rate that the volcanic islands were sinking.

Charles Darwin proposed such an origin for atolls in 1842 based on his expeditions on the *Beagle* from 1831 to 1836. He suggested that volcanic islands were first formed with their peaks exposed above sea level. At this stage, coral reefs were established as fringing reef complexes around the volcanic island. He posited that with time the volcanic islands subsided and were eroded, but that the growth of the coral reefs was able to keep up with the subsidence. In this way, as the volcanic islands sank below sea level, the coral reefs continued to grow and eventually formed a ring circling the location of the former volcanic island. When Darwin proposed this theory in 1842 he did not know that ancient eroded volcanic mountains underlay the atolls he studied. More than 100 years later, drilling confirmed his prediction that volcanic rocks would be found beneath the coralline rocks on several atolls.

With the advent of plate tectonics in the 1970s, the cause of the subsidence of the volcanoes became apparent. When oceanic crust is created at mid-ocean ridges, it is typically about 1.7 miles (2.7 km) below sea level. With time, as the oceanic crust moves away from the mid-ocean ridges, it cools and contracts, sinking to about 2.5 miles (4 km) below sea level. In many places on the seafloor, small volcanoes form on the oceanic crust a short time after the main part of the crust formed at the mid-ocean ridge. These volcanoes may stick above sea level a few hundred meters. As the oceanic crust moves away from the mid-ocean ridges, these volcanoes subside below sea level. If the volcanoes happen to be in the tropics where corals can grow, and if the rate of subsidence is slow enough for the growth of coral to keep up with subsidence, then atolls may form where the volcanic island used to be. If corals do not grow or cannot keep up with subsidence, then the island subsides below sea level and the top of the island gets scoured by wave erosion, forming a flat-topped mountain that continues to subside below sea level. These flat-topped mountains are known as guyots, many of which were mapped during exploration of the seafloor associated with military operations of World War II.

Reefs are extremely sensitive and diverse environments, and cannot tolerate large changes in temperature, pollution, turbidity, or water depth. Reefs have also been subject to mining, destruction for navigation, and even sites of testing of nuclear bombs in the Pacific. Thus, human-induced and natural changes to the shoreline environment pose a significant threat to the reef environment.

Conclusion

The coastal zone contains an amazingly diverse suite of different environments, including those on depositional shorelines, and those on erosional shores. Beaches show a zonation from the foreshore, through backshore and storm ridge, and may be followed inland by coastal cliffs, forest, dunes, lagoons, or coastal wetlands. Barrier islands are elongate ridges of sand that are detached from the mainland, and elongate parallel to the coast. They are typically cut by tidal inlets that allow passage of water, ships, and organisms between the open ocean and the back-barrier environment. Lagoons, bays, and sounds separate the mainland from barrier islands that are long narrow offshore beaches. Barrier islands are common along the East Coast of the United States (e.g., south shore of Long Island; Atlantic City, New Jersey; Outer Banks, North Carolina; and Galveston, Texas).

Estuaries are transitional environments between rivers and the sea, where freshwater mixes with seawater and are influenced by tides. Most were formed when sea levels were lower, and rivers carved out deep valleys that are now flooded by water. They are typically bordered by tidal wetlands and intertidal flats, and are sensitive ecological zones that are prone to disturbances by pollution, storms, and overuse by people.

Deltas are depositional systems that form at the mouths of rivers, and show a diversity of forms related to the relative strength of sediment supply, waves, and currents in moving sand. The delta front environment is dominated by marine conditions, and is prone to rapid subsidence and is very sensitive to sea-level rise. The delta plain is a coastal extension of the river system comprised of river and overbank sedimentary deposits, typically comprised of flat meandering streams and their flood plains.

Glaciated coasts are of two main types, including those formed by mountain glaciers that came to the sea forming deeply eroded fiords with small moraine deposits at their mouths, and coasts that have experienced continental glaciations. The latter typically has rocky shorelines with many promontories and embayments, and may have huge terminal moraine deposits marking where the glaciers made their furthest advance. (Long Island and Cape Cod are examples of terminal moraines.)

Reefs are organic framework-supported wave-resistant mounds built by a variety of organisms including corals. They represent very fragile environments that cannot withstand changes to water purity, temperature, or physical disturbance, and represent a very threatened environment by coastal development. Reefs are of several types, including barrier reefs that grow offshore on some coasts such as northeastern Australia, and atolls that form circular rings around islands in the tropics that have mostly subsided below sea level.

2

Origin of Coastal Hazards: Coastal Processes

The highly variable environments found along coastlines as described in the previous chapter are shaped by a combination of different processes including waves, tides, storms, and in geologically recent times, humankind's changes to the shoreline environment. Most of the time, these processes operate at levels that are predictable, expected, and form part of the daily rhythm of life on the coasts, but other times these processes can impart dramatic changes very quickly, and sometimes pose great hazards to coastal residents. To appreciate and mitigate the hazards posed by living along coastlines, the processes that affect the interaction of the land, water, and atmosphere in this critical, dynamic and ever-changing environment must be understood. There are several major factors that influence the development and potential of hazards along the coastline, including waves, tides, storms, and human-induced changes to the shoreline. These are each discussed in turn in this chapter, using examples of where each pose significant hazards. Following chapters discuss how rising sea levels affect these processes, and give examples of when these natural, sometimes hazardous processes have become disasters because people have moved into their way without understanding the threat they pose.

Waves

Waves are the most important contributor of energy to the shoreline, and thus constitute the most important process for understanding coastal changes and evolution. Waves are generated by winds that blow across the water surface. The frictional drag of the wind on the surface transfers energy from the air to the sea, which become expressed as waves. These waves may travel great distances across entire ocean basins and they may be thought of as energy in motion. This energy is released or transferred to the shoreline when the waves crash on the beach. Over time, this energy is able to move entire beaches and erode cliffs grain-by-grain, slowly but dramatically changing the appearance of the beach environment.

The amount of energy transferred from ocean waves to the coast is surprisingly large. For instance, if waves averaging one to three feet (0.3–1 m) in height strike a coastline, the amount of energy transferred to every 250-mile (400-km) long segment of the shoreline is about equal to the amount of energy produced by a typical nuclear power plant. If the waves are larger, the amount of energy transferred by the waves increases rapidly. This is because wave energy is proportional to the square (exponent) of the wave height, such that if the waves are increased by a factor of two from three to six feet (~1 to 2 m), then the amount of energy transferred to the coast will be increased by a factor of four (2 × 2). The remarkable amount of energy transferred in the coastal environment is awe inspiring, and can be appreciated by watching waves crash into headlands from many coastal cliffs. Even the sound of the waves crashing against the cliffs represents significant transfer of energy from the ocean to the coastal atmosphere. Someday it may be possible to harness some of this energy to be used to power cities, thus reducing use of polluting fossil fuels.

When waves are generated by winds over deep water they develop a characteristic spacing and height, known as the *wavelength* and *height*. The wave crest is the highest part of the wave, and the wave trough is the low point between waves. Wavelength is the distance between successive crests or troughs, the wave height is the vertical distance between troughs and crests, and *amplitude* is one-half of the wave height. *Wave fronts* are (imaginary) lines drawn parallel to the wave crests, and the wave moves perpendicular to the wave fronts. The time (in seconds) that it takes successive wave crests to pass a point is known as the wave period.

The height, wavelength and period of waves is determined by how strong the wind is that generates the waves, how long it blows for, and the distance over which the wind blows (known as the *fetch*). The longer and stronger and the greater the distance the wind blows over, the

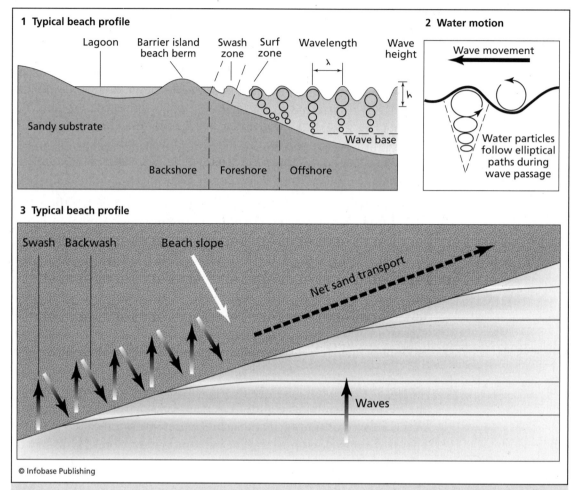

1 Typical beach profile

Lagoon   Barrier island   Swash   Surf   Wavelength   Wave
          beach berm   zone   zone   height

λ

h

Sandy substrate

Wave base

Backshore | Foreshore | Offshore

2 Water motion

Wave movement

Water particles
follow elliptical
paths during
wave passage

3 Typical beach profile

Swash Backwash   Beach slope

Net sand transport

Waves

© Infobase Publishing

Diagram of wave train (1, 2) showing wave motion, illustrating orbital paths followed by water particles. Note that wave motion dies out at a distance equal to half the wavelength of the waves, known as the wave base. When the wave base encounters the seafloor, friction slows down the motion of the wave and distorts its shape, causing the wave to crash on the beach. (3) Waves that hit the beach at an angle cause the water and sand particles to be washed up the beachface obliquely. When the backwash moves the water and sand particles back down the beachface, gravity moves the particles parallel to the beachface slope. The net effect is that the swash/backwash action on beaches moves sand particles down the beachface, sometimes half a mile (hundreds of m) per day.

longer the wavelength, the greater the wave height, and the longer the period.

It is important to remember that waves are energy in motion, and the water in the waves does not travel along with the waves. The motion of individual water particles as a wave passes form a roughly circular orbit that decreases in radius with depth below the wave. Swimmers experience this motion while bobbing in waves in the ocean, as their

Waves at Mossel Bay, South Africa: View of 12th green with 18th hole and clubhouse of The Caves Course at Pinnacle Point Beach and Golf Resort *(Getty Images)*

bodies move roughly up and down or in a circular path as the waves pass their location. The energy passes with the wave, but the swimmer just bobs up and down in response to the passage of the wave.

The motion of water particles in waves changes as the water depth decreases and the waves approach shore. At a depth known as the *wave base*, equal to roughly one-half of the wavelength, the circular motion induced by the wave begins to feel the sea bottom, which exerts a frictional drag on the wave. This changes the circular particle paths to elliptical paths, and causes the upper part of the wave to move ahead of the deeper parts. Eventually, the wave becomes over-steepened and begins to break, as the wave crashes into shore in the surf zone. In this surf zone, the water is actually moving forward, causing the common erosion, transportation, and deposition of sand along beaches.

Most coastlines are irregular and have many headlands, bays, bends, and changes in water depth from place to place. These variables cause waves that are similar in deep water to approach the shoreline differently in different places. On many beaches, waves may come ashore gently in one place yet form large breakers down the beach. These changes can be attributed to changes in the underwater slope of the seabed and the shape of the beach. *Wave refraction* occurs when a straight wave front approaches a shoreline obliquely. The part of the wave front that first feels shallow water (with a depth of less than one-half of the wavelength, known as the wave base) begins to slow down while the rest of the wave continues at its previous velocity. This causes the wave front to bend, or be refracted. This effect tends to cause waves to bend towards headlands, concentrating energy in those places, and to concentrate less energy in bays. Material is eroded from the headlands, and transported to and deposited in the bays.

When waves approach a beach obliquely, a similar phenomenon to the refraction of the wave fronts around headlands occurs. This bending of the wave fronts causes waves that approach at high angles to bend into arriving headlong into the beachface. Even though the waves are refracted, they may still crash onto the beach obliquely, moving sand particles sideways up the beach with each wave. As the wave returns to the sea in the backwash, the wave energy has been transferred to the shoreline (and has moved the sand grains), and gravity is the driving force moving the water and sand, which then moves the particles directly downhill. The net result is that sand particles move obliquely up and straight down the beach slope, moving slightly sideways along the beach with each passing wave. This process commonly moves individual sand grains in the swash and backwash zone almost a mile (1.6 km) per day along beaches, in a phenomenon known as longshore drift. If the supply or transportation route of the sand particles is altered by human activity, such as the construction of sea walls or groins, the beach will respond by dramatically changing in some way, as discussed in the following sidebar.

Wave Erosion of Coastal Cliffs at Plymouth, Massachusetts

The town of Plymouth, Massachusetts, is located between Cape Cod and Boston, and has many high coastal cliffs composed largely of old glacial deposits. These cliffs are being actively eroded at a rate of a few inches to a few tens of feet per year, and the residents and communities have attempted a wide variety of techniques to try to eliminate or reduce the erosion. So far all have failed, and houses perched on top of the coastal cliffs continue to lose acreage and eventually fall down the cliffs onto the beach. Some of the efforts of local residents to prevent erosion on their property have actually compounded the problems for the area as a whole. For instance, some residents have built seawalls on their property, others have constructed jetties, and others have built fences or planted vegetation to try to cut the erosion from runoff. While each of these may temporarily deflect the energy away from their properties, the total energy received on the beach is the same and must be accepted elsewhere. Deflection of energy in one place leads to its concentration elsewhere.

When seawalls are built in one small, restricted area but not adjacent areas, the rate of erosion on the coastal cliffs may actually be increased, because the energy that hits the wall is reflected downward and removes sand from the beach in front of the wall. The waves also hit the edges of the wall and severely erode the unprotected adjacent cliff section. The erosion induced by the seawall eventually causes the beach in front of it to become steeper and narrower, which allows bigger waves to run up the now narrower beach, crashing directly into the wall. This will eventually destroy the wall, after repeated pounding by waves, sand,

ROGUE WAVES

Most ocean waves travel in sets with each wave having a rather uniform height, wavelength, and velocity. Every once in a while, however, an unusual isolated wave with an exceptionally large height may move across the ocean, and wash up on shore. These waves, known as rogue waves, are exceptionally rare but can be very destructive. Every year a few rogue waves wash onto beaches somewhere in the world, often sweeping unsuspecting swimmers to sea, never to be seen again. Other rogue waves are suspected of sinking ships without a trace while they are at sea. Many maritime legends, such as reports of disappearing ships in the Bermuda Triangle, may actually result from localized interactions of ocean current with seasonal winds, producing the so-far unpredictable rogue waves.

How do rogue waves form? Waves usually lose energy and decrease in amplitude as they interact with other waves as they move away from the region in which they were generated. In some cases, however, waves interact with currents in a way that dramatically increases the amplitude of some isolated waves, forming huge towering wave crests capable of capsizing even the largest of ships. Some of these rogue waves have been reported to be hundreds of feet high. Regions where large ocean swells meet strong oncoming currents are known for rogue waves. For instance, off the coast of southern Africa, huge ocean swells generated in the southern ocean between Africa and Antarctica move north, and meet the south flowing Aghullas current flowing out of the Mozambique Channel. The current causes some of the waves to become steeper and shorter in wavelength, with some becoming so steep they are close to breaking in open waters. Deep holes often form in front of these waves, presenting a particular hazard to ships as the holes can often not be seen until the ship is plunging into the depths, only to be quickly overrun by the towering wave. Huge rogue waves are known to form in regions such as the north Atlantic, and near Bermuda where large ocean swells interact with the Gulf Stream current. Rogue waves may be the explanation for the large number of ships that have been reported lost without a trace in the Bermuda Triangle region.

and rocks. In time, the cliffs erode behind the seawall, causing it to collapse.

Other residents have constructed fences to try to reduce the velocity of the waves, but these are typically washed away by the first nor'easter. Still other attempts have focused on protecting the cliffs with vegetation, or building pipes and drainages for water to flow away from the cliffs without enhancing the erosion.

All of these attempts have locally and temporarily slowed the erosion of the cliffs, but over the course of many years they have been insignificant or have even accelerated erosion. These problems and attempts at solutions are not unique to Plymouth—many places in New England and Cape Cod, and coasts around the world have similar problems and many others, yet none have been able to completely halt the erosion.

Coastal cliff erosion at Plymouth, Massachusetts. Made of sand and gravel deposited by glaciers, the cliffs are being eroded by waves. *(T. Kusky)*

Tides

Tides are the periodic rise and fall of the ocean surface, and alternate submersion and exposure of the intertidal zone along coasts. Currents caused by the rise and fall of the sea surface are the strongest currents in the ocean, and were attributed to the gravitational effects of the Sun and

Residents of Plymouth, Massachusetts, try to reduce coastal cliff erosion by constructing a hodgepodge of different cliff reinforcements. This is an ineffective strategy since the rock walls deflect energy down and erode the beach causing the walls to collapse, and waves can work around the discontinuous walls, collapsing them from behind, and enhancing erosion elsewhere. These two photos show rock walls, nets, vegetation, and sand fences all erected as deterrents to cliff erosion. *(T. Kusky)*

Moon since at least the times of Pliny the Elder (23–79 c.e.). In some places, currents induced by tides are the most significant factor controlling development of the beach and shoreline environment. These places include tidal inlets, passages between islands and the mainland, and areas with exceptionally large tidal ranges (e.g., Bay of Fundy, Gulf of Alaska, and Cook Inlet, North Sea). Tides are responsible for depositing deltas on the lagoonal and oceanward sides of tidal inlets, and for moving large amounts of sediment in regions with high tidal ranges.

The range in sea surface height between the high and low is known as the *tidal range,* and this varies considerably from barely detectable to more than 50 feet (15 m). Most places have two high tides and two low tides each tidal day, in a period of about 24 hours and 50 minutes, corresponding to the time between successive passes of the Moon over any point. The tidal period is the time between successive high or successive low tides. Places with two high and two low tides per day have semidaily, or semidiurnal tides. Fewer places have only one high and one low tide per day, a cycle referred to as a diurnal or daily tide. Semidiurnal tides are often not equal in heights between the two highs and two lows.

Spring tides are those that occur near the full and new Moons, and have a tidal range larger than the mean tidal range. In contrast, *neap tides* occur during the first and third quarters of the Moon, and are characterized by lower than average tidal ranges.

Sir Isaac Newton was the first to publicly and clearly elucidate the mechanics of tides, and how they are related to the gravitational attraction of the Moon. In his equilibrium theory of tides he assumed a non-rotating Earth, covered with water and having no continents. In this simplified model aimed at understanding the origin of tides, gravitational attraction pulls the Earth and Moon toward each other, while centrifugal forces act in the opposite direction and keep them apart. Since the Moon is so much smaller than the Earth, the center of mass and rotation of the Earth-Moon system is located within the Earth 2,900 miles (4,670 km) from the Earth's center, on the side of the Earth closest to the Moon. This causes unbalanced forces since a unit of water on the Earth's surface closest to the Moon is located 59 Earth radii (233,015 miles; 375,830 km) from the Moon's surface, whereas a unit of water on the opposite side of the Earth is located 61 Earth radii (240,913 miles; 388,570 km) from the nearest point on the Moon. Since the force of gravity is inversely proportional to the distance squared between the two points, the Moon's gravitational pull is much greater for the unit of

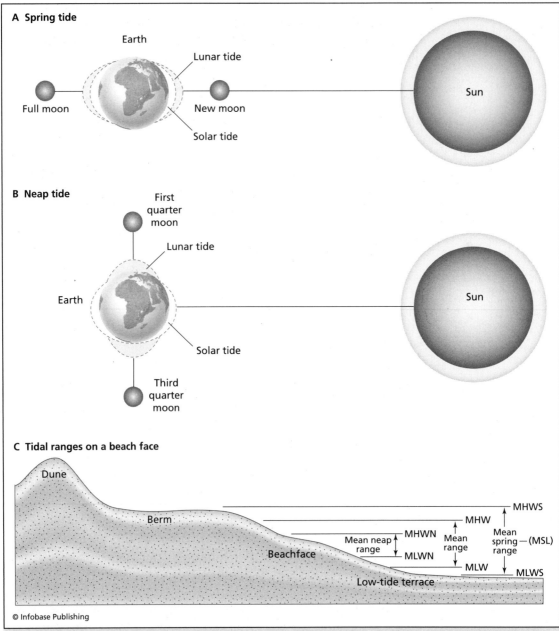

A Spring tide

Earth

Lunar tide

Full moon

New moon

Solar tide

Sun

B Neap tide

First quarter moon

Lunar tide

Earth

Solar tide

Sun

Third quarter moon

C Tidal ranges on a beach face

Dune

Berm

Beachface

Mean neap range

MHWN

MLWN

Mean range

MHWS

MHW

Mean spring — (MSL) range

MLW

MLWS

Low-tide terrace

© Infobase Publishing

Diagram explaining the formation of tides. The size of the tidal bulge and the tidal range are determined by the relative alignment of the Earth, Moon and Sun. Both the Moon and Sun pull the water of the planet into separate tidal bulges. During periods of full Moon and new Moon (A), the Earth, Sun, and Moon are all aligned and the tidal bulges are additive producing large tides known as spring tides. During first and third quarter Moon phases the Sun, Moon, and Earth are out of alignment (B), and the tidal bulges are subtractive, producing smaller tidal ranges known as neap tides. (C) shows the different relationships between these tidal ranges on a beach. The spring tides have the greatest tidal range, and the neap tides have the smallest range. Both tides range above and below mean sea level (MSL). (MHW = mean high water, MLW = mean low water, S = spring, N = neap). *(Modified after Davis and Fitzgerald, 2004)* water closer to the Moon. However, *centrifugal forces* that act perpendicular to the axis of rotation of the Earth also affect the tides, and must be added with the gravitational forces to yield a vector sum that is the tide-producing force. Together these forces result in the gravitational force of the Moon exceeding the centrifugal force on the side of Earth closest to the Moon, drawing water in a bulge toward the Moon. On the opposite side of the Earth the centrifugal force overbalances the gravitational attraction of the Moon, so there the water is essentially dragged away from the Earth.

The interaction of the gravitational forces and centrifugal forces creates a more complex pattern of tides on Newton's model Earth. Directly beneath the Moon and on the opposite side of the Earth, both the gravitational force and the centrifugal force act perpendicular to the surface, but elsewhere the vector sum of the two forces is not perpendicular to the surface. The result of adding the centrifugal force and gravity vectors is a two-sided, egg-shaped bulge that points toward and away from the Moon. Newton called these bulges the equilibrium tide. The situation is however even more complex, since the Sun also exerts a gravitational attraction on the Earth and its water, forming an additional egg-shaped bulge that is about 0.46 times as large as the lunar tidal bulge.

If we consider the Earth to be rotating through the tidal bulges on a water-covered planet, the simplest situation arises with two high tides and two low tides each day, since the lunar tides dominate over the effects of the solar tides. However, the Earth has continents that hinder the equal flow of water, and bays and estuaries that trap and amplify the tides in certain places; in addition, frictional drag slows the passage of the tidal bulge through shallow waters. These obstacles cause the tides to be different at different places on the Earth, explaining the large range in observed tidal ranges and periods.

Tidal waves (not tsunamis) travel at 435 miles (700 km) per hour in the open ocean, but are slowed by their interactions with continental landmasses, islands, and other features. As the tidal bulge moves onto the continental shelves, it experiences friction from the shallow water, and slows to as little a 6–12 miles (10–20 km) per hour. This causes the water in the tidal crest to essentially pile up and steepen the shape of the bulge, and quadruple its height from about 1–2 feet (0.3–.61 m) in the open ocean to 9–10 feet (2.7–3 m) on many open shorelines.

In addition, the *Coriolis force* must be taken into account as tides involve considerable movement of water from one place to another. The Coriolis force arises because the surface of the Earth at the equator is rotating through space faster than points on and near the poles. Thus, when water or air moves toward the pole it is moving faster than the new solid ground beneath it, causing objects to be deflected to the right in the Northern Hemisphere, and to the left in the Southern Hemisphere. Currents such as the Gulf Stream follow this deflection, and tides are also influenced by the Coriolis force, causing the tidal bulge to effectively rotate in a counterclockwise way in the Northern Hemisphere, and clockwise in the Southern Hemisphere.

Unusual mushroom-shaped seastacks caused by high tidal ranges at Hopewell Rocks, New Brunswick, Canada *(Shutterstock)*

The shapes of coastlines can have a strong influence on the character of tides. Funnel-shaped embayments, estuaries, and coves cause tidal waves to become constricted as the water is forced into a progressively smaller area, forcing the wave to become taller, steeper, and in some cases to form a breaking wave known as a bore that migrates up the bay as the tide floods the bay. The world's largest *tidal bores* are found in the Bay of Fundy where the tidal range reaches more than 52 feet (16 m) in height at the head of the bay. In this location, the tidal bore comes in as a rapidly moving wave, moving up the bay and even moving up local rivers causing them to run backwards. Some of the largest and fastest tidal bores occur in China and South America, where the tide has a lower range but comes in faster. The bores on the Qiantang River in northern China, and on the Araguari River in South America have heights of up to 16 feet (5 m) and move at rates of 12.5 miles (20 km) per hour, allowing adventurists to surf these bores. Other large tidal bores are known from the Seine estuary in France, Cook Inlet and Bristol Bay in Alaska, Gulf of Cambay in Australia, and the Río de la Plata estuary in South America.

Tides in Turnagain Arm, Alaska

Tidal currents can be hazardous, particularly to those who may not be familiar with an area and not know the tidal range and the speed at which the incoming tides can fill an area. A good example of the hazards associated with tidal currents is provided by parts of Cook Inlet, Alaska. Just outside of Anchorage, a part of Cook Inlet known as Turnagain Arm has tidal ranges in the 30–35 foot (9–10.7 m) range. At low tides,

Turnagain Arm consists of mudflats with tidal channels, and when the tide comes in, it typically does so with a tidal bore, or wave front that moves quite rapidly up the drowned fiord, faster than a person can run. The mud that forms the tidal flats is composed largely of glacial flour, a mixture of mud and fine silt that has some unusual properties. The mud is *thixotropic,* meaning that it appears to be fairly rigid when it is held or is still, but when it is shaken or disturbed, it rapidly turns into a fluid. Every year, tourists or other unsuspecting residents walk out onto the mud, which can suddenly start to grip your boots. Most people's reaction is to wiggle to get loose, but this only makes the mud more fluid, and causes the person to sink further into the mud. The mud surrounds the person, and has an incredibly strong suction force such that makes it virtually impossible to pull the person out of the mud without tearing off their limbs. One possible way to escape is seek emergency assistance to pump water next to the person, and remove them with a helicopter. But Turnagain Arm is fairly remote, even though it is close to a major city, and it takes time for emergency crews to arrive. The tides are fast, and they come in at 20–40 miles (32.2–64.4 km) per hour, and quickly rise many feet, drowning the person stuck in the mud.

Storms

Storms can cause some of the most dramatic and rapid changes to the coastal zones, and represent one of the major, most unpredictable hazards to people living along coastlines. Storms include hurricanes, which form in the late summer and fall, and extratropical lows, which form in

Tidal bore in the Bay of Fundy, Canada, along the Maccan River *(Alamy)*

the late fall through spring. Hurricanes originate in the tropics and for North America, migrate westward and northwestward before turning back to the northeast to return to the cold North Atlantic, weakening the storm. North Atlantic hurricanes are driven to the west by the trade winds, and bend to the right because the Coriolis force makes moving objects curve to the right in the Northern Hemisphere. Hurricane paths are further modified by other weather conditions, such as the location of high and low pressure systems, and their interaction with weather fronts. Extratropical lows (also known as coastal storms, and nor'easters in New England) move eastward across North America, and typically intensify when they hit the Atlantic and move up the coast. Both types of storms rotate counterclockwise and the low pressure at the centers of the storms raises the water several to several tens of feet. This extra water moves ahead of the storms as a storm surge that represents an additional height of water above the normal tidal range. The wind from the storms adds further height to the storm surge, with the total height of the storm surge being determined by the length, duration, and direction of wind, plus how low the pressure gets in the center of the storm. The most destructive storm surges are those that strike low-lying communities at high tide, as the effects of the storm surge and the regular astronomical tides are cumulative. Add high winds and large waves on top of the storm surge, and coastal storms and hurricanes are seen as very powerful agents of destruction. They are capable of removing entire beaches and rows of homes, causing great amounts of cliff erosion and significant redistribution of sands in dunes and the back-beach environment. Very precise prediction of the height and timing of the approach of the storm surge is necessary to warn coastal residents of when they need to evacuate, and when they may not need to leave their homes.

Formation and Characteristics of Hurricanes

Intense tropical storms with sustained winds of more than 74 MPH (119 km/hr) are known as hurricanes if they form in the northern Atlantic or eastern Pacific Oceans, cyclones if they form in the Indian Ocean or near Australia, and typhoons if they form in the western North Pacific Ocean. Most large hurricanes have a central eye with calm or light winds and clear skies or broken clouds, surrounded by an eye wall, a ring of very tall and intense thunderstorms that spin around the eye, with some of the most intense winds and rain of the entire storm system. The eye is surrounded by spiral rain bands that spin counterclockwise in the Northern Hemisphere (clockwise in the Southern Hemisphere) in toward the eye wall, moving faster and generating huge waves as they approach the center. Wind speeds increase toward the center of the storm and the atmospheric pressure decreases to a low in the eye, uplifting the sea surface in the storm center. Surface air flows in toward the eye of the hurricane, then moves upward, often above nine miles (15 km), along the eye wall. From there it moves outward in a large outflow, until it descends outside the spiral rain bands. Air in the rain bands is ascending, whereas between the rain bands, belts of descending air counter this flow. Air in the very center of the eye descends to the surface. Hurricanes drop enormous amounts of precipitation, typically spawn numerous tornadoes, and cause intense coastal damage from winds, waves, and storm surges, where the sea surface may be elevated up to 20 or more feet (6 m) above its normal level.

Most hurricanes form in the summer and early fall over warm tropical waters when the winds are light and the humidity is high. In the North Atlantic, hurricane season generally runs from June through November, when the tropical surface waters are warmer than 80°F (26.5°C). They typically begin when a group of unorganized thunderstorms are acted on by some trigger that causes the air to begin converging and spinning. These triggers are found in the intertropical convergence zone

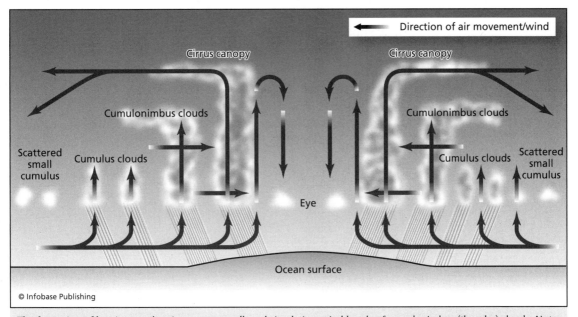

The formation of hurricanes, showing eye, eye wall, and circulating spiral bands of cumulonimbus (thunder) clouds. Note that the sea surface elevation is higher in the center of the storm from the low pressure within the eye.

that separates the northeast trade winds in the Northern Hemisphere from the southeast trade winds in the Southern Hemisphere. Most hurricanes form within this zone, between 5° and 20° latitude. When a low-pressure system develops in this zone during hurricane season, the isolated thunderstorms can develop into an organized convective system that strengthens to form a hurricane. Many Atlantic hurricanes form in a zone of weak convergence on the eastern side of tropical waves that form over North Africa, then move westward where they intensify over warm tropical waters.

In order for hurricanes to develop, high-level winds must be minor, otherwise they would disperse the tops of the growing thunderclouds. In addition, high-level winds must not be descending, since this would also inhibit the upward growth of the thunderstorms. Once the mass of thunderstorms is organized, hurricanes gain energy from evaporating water from the warm tropical oceans. When the water vapor condenses inside the thunderclouds, this heat energy is then converted to wind energy. The upper-level clouds then move outward, causing the storm to grow stronger, and decreasing the pressure in the center of the storm. The low pressure in the storm's center draws the outlying thunderstorms in toward the surface low, and these rain bands then spiral inward because of the Coriolis force. The clouds spin progressively faster as they move inward, because of the conservation of angular momentum.

The strength of hurricanes is measured using the *Saffir-Simpson scale,* which measures the damage potential of a storm, considering such factors as the central barometric pressure, maximum sustained wind speeds, and the potential height of the storm surge. Category 1 hurricanes have central pressures of greater than 980 millibars, sustained winds between 74 and 95 MPH (119–153 km/hr), and a likely four to five foot (1–1.5 m) storm surge. Damage potential is minimal, with likely effects including downed power lines, ruined crops, and minor damage to weak parts of buildings. Category 2 hurricanes have central barometric pressures between 979 and 965 millibars, maximum sustained winds between 96 and 110 MPH (155–177 km/hr), and six-to-eight-foot (1.8–2.4 m) storm surges. Damage is typically moderate, including roof and chimney damage, beached and splintered boats, destroyed crops, road signs, and traffic lights. Category 3 hurricanes have central barometric pressures falling between 964 and 945 millibars, sustained winds between 111 and 130 MPH (179–209 km/hr), and storm surges between nine and 12 feet (2.7–3.6 m). Category 3 hurricanes are major storms capable of extensive property damage including uprooting large trees,

Development in Miami Beach, Florida. Buildings on oceanfront are prone to being hit by large tidal surges with 30-foot (9-m) waves on top, and hurricane force winds. *(Shutterstock)*

and the destruction of mobile homes and poorly constructed coastal houses. Category 4 storms can be devastating, with central barometric pressures falling between 940 and 920 millibars, sustained winds between 131 and 155 MPH (211–249 km/hr), and storm surges between 13 and 18 feet (4–5.5 m). These storms typically rip the roofs off homes, and businesses, destroy sea piers, and throw boats well inland. Waves may breach sea walls causing large-scale coastal flooding. Category 5 storms are truly massive with central barometric pressures, dropping below 920 millibars, maximum sustained winds above 155 MPH (249 km/hr), and storm surges over 18 feet (5.5 m). Storms with this power rarely hit land but when they do they are capable of leveling entire towns, moving large amounts of coastal sediments, and causing large death tolls.

Many cyclones are spawned in the Indian Ocean. Bangladesh is a densely populated low-lying country, sitting mostly at or near sea level, between India and Myanmar. It is a delta environment, built where the Ganges and Brahmaputra Rivers drop their sediment eroded from the Himalaya Mountains. It sits directly in the path of many Bay of Bengal tropical cyclones, and has been hit by seven of the nine most deadly hurricane disasters in the history of the world. On November 12 and 13 of 1970, a Category 5 typhoon hit Bangladesh with 155 MPH (249.5 km/hr) winds, and a 23-foot (7-m) high storm surge that struck at the astronomically high tides of a full moon. The result was devastating, with 400,000 human deaths and half a million farm animals perishing.

Again in 1990, another cyclone hit the same area, this time with a 20-foot (6-m) storm surge and 145 MPH (233 km/hr) winds, killing another 140,000 people and another half-million farm animals.

The Gulf of Mexico coast, Florida, and the southeastern United States are generally affected by several hurricanes every season from late summer through fall. Hurricane Andrew was the most destructive hurricane in United State's history prior to Hurricane Katrina in 2005, causing more than $30 billion in damage in August 1992. Andrew crossed Florida as a Category 4 hurricane, and came ashore with a 17-foot (5.2-m) storm surge, and winds that destroyed or damaged 135,000 buildings. In 2005, Hurricanes Katrina and Rita devastated much of the Gulf coast of Louisiana, including New Orleans, and neighboring Mississippi. Although Katrina only landed as a Category 3 storm, it was a large storm with a high tidal surge. This, combined with factors such as unappreciated natural subsidence of the city of New Orleans, and a levee system that had not yet been adequately repaired since the 1969 hurricane damage of Hurricane Camille, led Katrina to become the most costly natural disaster in United States history. These hurricanes are described in detail in a later chapter.

Extratropical Cyclones

Extratropical cyclones, also known as wave cyclones, are hurricane-strength storms that form in middle and high latitudes at all times of the year. Examples of these strong storms include the famous nor'easters of New England, storms along the east slopes of the Rockies, disturbances in the Gulf of Mexico, and smaller hurricane-strength storms that form in arctic regions. These storms develop along polar fronts that form semicontinuous boundaries between cold polar air and warm subtropical air. Troughs of low pressure can develop along these polar fronts, and winds that blow in opposite directions to the north and south of the low set up a cyclonic (counterclockwise in the Northern Hemisphere) wind shear that can cause a wavelike kink to develop in the front. This kink is an incipient cyclone, and includes (in the Northern Hemisphere) a cold front that pushes southward and counterclockwise, and a warm front that spins counterclockwise and moves to the north. A comma-shaped band of precipitation develops around a central low that forms where the cold and warm fronts meet, and the whole system will migrate east or northeast along the polar front, driven by high-altitude steering winds.

The energy for extratropical cyclones to develop and intensify comes from warm air rising and cold air sinking, transferring potential energy into kinetic energy. Condensation also provides extra energy as latent heat. These storms can intensify rapidly, and are especially strong when the cold front overtakes the warm front, occluding the system. The point where the cold front, warm front, and occluded front meet is known as a triple point and is often the site of the formation of a new secondary low-pressure system to the east or southeast of the main front. This new secondary low often develops into a new cyclonic system and moves east or northeastward, and may become the stronger of the two lows. In the case of New England's nor'easters, the secondary lows typically develop off the coast of the Carolinas or Virginia, then rapidly intensify as they move up the coast, bringing cyclonic winds and moisture in from the northeast off the Atlantic Ocean.

Effects of Storms and Hurricanes

Some of the most rapid and severe damage to coastal regions is inflicted by hurricanes, and these storms are responsible for the largest numbers of deaths in coastal disasters. The number of deaths from hurricanes has been reduced dramatically in recent years with our increased ability to forecast the strength and landfall of hurricanes, and our ability to monitor their progress with satellites. However, the costs of hurricanes in terms of property damage has greatly increased, as more and more people build expensive homes along the coast. The greatest number of deaths from hurricanes has been from effects of the storm surge. Storm surges typically come ashore as a wall of water that rushes onto land at the forward velocity of the hurricane, as the storm waves on top of the surge are pounding the coastal area with additional energy. For instance, when Hurricane Camille hit Mississippi in 1969 with 200 MPH (322 km/hr) winds, a 24-foot (7.3-m) high storm surge moved into coastal areas, killing most of the 256 people that perished in this storm. Winds and tornadoes account for more deaths. Heavy rains from hurricanes also cause considerable damage. Flooding and severe erosion is often accompanied by massive mudflows and debris avalanches, such as those caused by Hurricane Mitch in Central America in 1998. In a period of several days, Mitch dropped 25–75 inches (63.5–190.5 cm) of rain on Nicaragua and Honduras, initiating many mudslides that were the main cause of the more than 11,000 deaths from this single storm. One of the worst events was the filling and collapse of a *caldera* on Casitas volcano—when the caldera could hold no more water, it gave way sending mudflows (lahars) cascading down on several villages, killing 2,000 people.

Storm Surges

A storm surge is water that is pushed ahead of storms, and typically moves on land as exceptionally high tides in front of severe ocean storms such as hurricanes. Storms and storm surges can cause some of the most dramatic and rapid changes to the coastal zones, and represent one of the major, most unpredictable hazards to people living along coastlines. Storms that produce surges include hurricanes (which form in the late summer and fall), and extratropical lows (which form in the late fall through spring). Hurricanes originate in the Tropics and (for North America) migrate westward and northwestward before turning back to the northeast to return to the cold North Atlantic, weakening the storm. North Atlantic hurricanes are driven to the west by the trade winds, and bend to the right because the Coriolis force makes objects moving above Earth's surface appear to curve to the right in the Northern Hemisphere. Hurricane paths are further modified by other weather conditions, such as the location of high and low pressure systems, and their interaction with weather fronts. Extratropical lows (also known as coastal storms, and nor'easters) move eastward across North America, and typically intensify when they hit the Atlantic and move up the coast. Both types of storms rotate counterclockwise and the low pressure at the centers of the storms raises the water several to several tens of feet. This extra water moves ahead of the storms as a storm surge that represents an additional height of water above the normal tidal range. The wind from the storms adds further height to the storm surge, with the total height of the storm surge being determined by the length, duration, and direction of wind, as well as how low the pressure gets in the center of the storm. The most destructive storm surges are those that strike low-lying communities at high tide, as the effects of the storm surge and the regular astronomical tides are cumulative.

Like many natural catastrophic events, the heights of storm surges to strike a coastline are statistically predictable. If the height of the storm surges is plotted on a semilogarithmic plot, with the height plotted in a linear interval and the frequency (in years) plotted on a logarithmic scale, then a linear slope results. What this means is that communities can plan for storm surges of a certain height to occur once every 50, 100, 300, or 500 years, although there is no way to predict when the actual storm surges will occur. It must be remembered that this is a long-term statistical average, and that one, two, three or more 500-year events may occur over a relatively short period, but averaged over a long time, the events average out to once every 500 years.

Storms are known to open new tidal inlets where none were previously (without regard to whether or not any homes were present in the path of the new tidal inlet), and to close inlets previously in existence. Storms also tend to remove large amounts of sand from the beachface and redeposit it in the deeper water offshore (below wave base), but this sand tends to gradually move back on to the beach in the intervals between storms when the waves are smaller. In short, storms are extremely effective modifiers of the beach environment, although they are unpredictable and dangerous.

Human-Induced Changes to the Shoreline

People are modifying the shoreline environment on a massive scale with the construction of new homes, resorts, and structures that attempt to reduce or prevent erosion along the beach. These modifications have been changing the dynamics of the beach in drastic ways, and most often, result in erosion and degradation of the beach. In many cases obstacles are constructed that disrupt the transportation of sand along the beach in longshore drift. This causes sand to build up at some locations, and to be removed from other locations further along the beach. Some of the worst culprits are *groins,* or walls of rock, concrete, or wood build at right angles to the shoreline that are designed to trap sand from longshore drift, and replenish a beach. The problem with groins is that they stop the longshore drift, causing the sand to accumulate on the updrift

Groin (rock jetty) sticking out into water. Notice how the beach is wide on one side of the wall, and depleted on the other side. *(Shutterstock)*

side, and to be removed from the downdrift side. Groins also set up conditions favorable for the formation of rip tides, which tend to take sand (and unsuspecting swimmers) offshore, out of the longshore drift system. The result of groin construction is typically a few triangular areas of sand next to rocky groins, along what was once a continuous beach. Little or no sand will remain in the areas on the downdrift sides of the groins. Therefore, when groins are constructed it usually becomes necessary to begin an expensive program of artificial replenishment of beach sands to fill in the areas that were eroded by the new pattern of longshore drift set up by the groins.

Construction or stabilization of inlets through barrier islands or beaches often includes the construction of jetties on either side of the channel, to prevent sand from entering and closing the channel. Like groins, these jetties prevent sand transportation by longshore drift, causing beaches to grow on the updrift side of the jetty. Sand that used to replenish the beach on the downdrift side gets blocked, or washed around the jetty into the tidal channel, where it moves into the lagoon to form tidal deltas. The result is that the beaches on the downdrift side of the jetties become sand-starved and thin, eventually disappearing.

Seawall along intercoastal waterway, West Palm Beach, Florida. Rocks were placed in front of seawall to reduce erosion of wall. Note the complete lack of sandy beach, since the seawall and rocks deflect the wave energy back to the beach removing the sand. *(CORBIS)*

Seawalls are also hazardous to maintaining a healthy beach. Seawalls have been constructed along many U.S. beaches in attempts to limit damage to buildings from high storm surges and waves. If a seawall is built along the base of a cliff at the backside of a beach, it may protect the cliff from erosion for some time, but it also accelerates erosion of the beach because it removes the source of sediment that previously replenished that beach. Eventually, the beach becomes narrower and lower, and the waves attack the seawall by undermining it until it collapses. If seawalls are only built along small sections of cliffs, such as along single plots owned by individual homeowners, the problems may

Waves crashing into seawall in Ventura County, California *(Photo Researchers, Inc.)*

be worse. Such is the case along the cliffs of Plymouth, Massachusetts. Waves will immediately attack the sides of the seawalls, causing accelerated erosion to the sea cliffs on either side of the seawall. This erosion will work its way behind the seawall causing it to collapse, and the result is that rates of erosion will actually be accelerated by the construction of the partial seawall. Seawalls have also been constructed along large sections of beaches by municipalities that suffered severe storm damage, and want to try to reduce the effects of the next storm. These extensive seawalls are a sentence of death for the beach, because they not only remove the source of sediment replenishment for the beach but they accelerate erosion by causing the wave energy to be reflected off the beach and down into the sand, causing it to be removed. Eventually, the erosion undermines the seawall, causing it to collapse.

Sand dunes in the backbeach area are naturally vegetated and covered with sea grasses and other plants. These dunes form a natural and effective barrier to high storm surges and waves, protecting the backbeach environment from the worst effects of these storms. Recreational overuse of many beaches has resulted in people trampling many of these grasses, or driving vehicles through them, creating many unvegetated paths and patches. When wind blows over these patches and paths, the wind removes sand from these areas in a process called deflation, resulting in a lowering of the dune height. When this happens, the dunes are no longer effective barriers for storm surges and waves, and the waves begin to wash over the dunes during storms. The storm waters will seek out the lowest point in the dune field and surge through this gap, deeply eroding a storm surge channel through the dunes. The result then is that the dunes are no longer able to protect the backbeach and lagoon from the storm's effects, and a storm channel and delta is formed from the sand that used to form the dunes.

Another human-induced change to the coastal environment results from the construction of dams along rivers that feed into the ocean. These rivers once fed sediment to the ocean, replenishing the beach. Since the dams have been built, there is more freshwater available for new coastal residents to drink, but the beaches are receiving less replenishment and are rapidly shrinking. The reservoirs behind the dams are filling up with the sediment that used to feed the beaches, so eventually the reservoirs will not be effective, and will have to be dredged (replenishing the beaches) or abandoned.

Longshore Sediment Transport and Management: Santa Barbara, California

Longshore drift of sand is strongly affected by changes to the beach, including the construction of groins and jetties. There are many examples of where groins were constructed, and beaches downdrift from the groins disappear. Likewise, there are many examples of where jetties were constructed at the ends of inlets, disrupting the flow of sand to the downdrift beaches, which gradually disappear. The sand that used to replenish these beaches either moves into the channel and forms deltas in the lagoon, or is carried to deep water by rip currents set up by the jetties.

One interesting example of the consequences of building jetties and breakwaters is provided by the boat harbor at Santa Barbara, California. In the downtown of scenic Santa Barbara, a beautiful harbor with many well cared for pleasure boats sits behind rock walls built as breakwaters, designed to keep large waves out of the harbor. The breakwaters, however, caused sand to build up forming a spit to the breakwaters, and then the spit continued to grow by longshore drift and the sand curved around the end of the spit filling the harbor with sand. Now the harbor needs nearly constant dredging to keep it navigable, and a dredging barge sweeps back and forth in the harbor, taking the sand from one side of the harbor entrance to the other, artificially keeping the process of longshore drift operating.

Conclusion

The coast is shaped by a variety of different forces, including long-term factors such as plate tectonics and sea level change, and short-term factors including waves, tides, and storms. In geologically recent times human-induced changes to the shoreline have changed the coastal environment dramatically, perhaps even more than the other main factors in some areas.

Waves are constantly scouring the coast, eroding cliffs, moving sand particles through longshore drift, and rearranging barrier islands and beaches. The amount of energy released by waves follows a square law, so large waves that are twice as high as smaller waves release four times as much energy as the smaller wave sets. Therefore, waves from storms and waves that form in the winter, when they tend to be larger, are much more powerful and erosive than the small waves that lap up on many beaches in the summer.

Tides are formed by a complex gravitational attraction of the Moon and Sun, displacing the water on the planet more than the solid Earth. Tidal wave crests move around the planet twice a day, and interact with coastlines in complex ways, causing tidal ranges to be amplified in some places, forming dangerous tidal bores and strong currents in tidal inlets.

Storms, and increased sea surface heights from storm surges, can do severe damage to the coast in short intervals of time. High winds and water levels, along with pounding waves from hurricanes and other storms have moved into many coastal areas, removing entire beaches, ripping up vegetation and destroying thousands of buildings. Hundreds of thousands of people have lost their lives in hurricanes along coastlines.

People have been changing the coastal environment dramatically in attempts to stabilize beaches, coastal cliffs, and make the beach environment more permanent. However, most of these attempts have only worked temporarily and many, if not most, have caused more severe damage elsewhere along beaches as a consequence of changing the beach dynamics. Beaches and coastlines are very dynamic environments that are always changing in response to a delicate balance between the forces of the sea, atmosphere and land. Any changes to this balance result in changes to the other parts of the system.

3

Effects of Rising Sea Levels and Coastal Subsidence

Sea level has risen and fallen by hundreds of feet many times in Earth history, and it is presently slowly rising at about one foot per century, but may be accelerating from the effects of global warming. The causes of sea-level rise and fall are complex and operate on vastly different time scales. These include growth and melting of glaciers, changes in the volume of the mid-ocean ridges, thermal expansion of water from global warming, and other complex interactions of the distribution of the continental landmass in mountains and plains during periods of faulting, mountain building, and basin forming activity. It is important to separate the local effects of the rising and sinking of the land known as relative sea level changes, from global changes in sea level that are referred to as eustatic events.

Sometimes individual large earthquakes may displace the land surface vertically, resulting in subsidence or uplift. One of the largest and best-documented cases of earthquake-induced subsidence resulted from the March 27, 1964, magnitude 9.2 earthquake in southern Alaska. This earthquake tilted a huge approximately 125,000 square mile (200,000 square km) area of the Earth's crust. Significant changes in ground level were recorded along the coast for more than 600 miles (1,000 km), including uplifts of up to 36 feet (11 m), subsidence of up to 6.5 feet (2 m), and lateral shifts of 5–50 feet. Much of the area that subsided was along Cook Inlet, north to Anchorage and Valdez, and south to Kodiak Island. Towns that were built around docks prior to the earthquake were suddenly located below the high tide mark, and entire

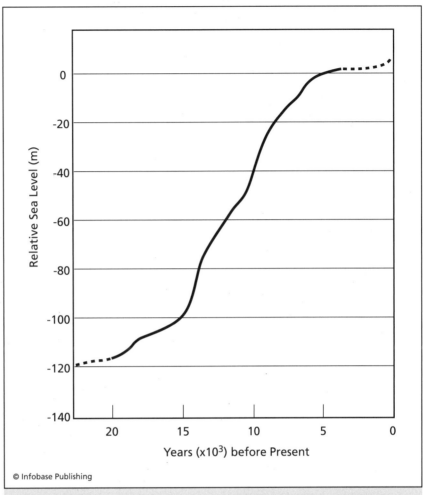

Graph showing short-term rising sea level since the last glacial period. Sea level rose quickly after the main continental ice sheets melted 20,000–10,000 years ago, slowed, and is now rising at about a foot (.3 m) per century, though possibly accelerating. *(NASA)*

towns had to move to higher ground. Forests that subsided found their root systems suddenly inundated by salt water, leading to the death of the forests. Populated areas located at previously safe distances from the high-tide (and storm) line became prone to flooding and storm surges, and had to be relocated.

The fastest changes in sea level are caused by instantaneous geologic catastrophes such as meteorite impacts into the ocean, but fortunately these types of events do not happen often. Seasonal changes can blow or move water to greater heights on one side of a basin, and lower on another side, cause water to expand and contract with changes in tem-

temperature, resulting in small changes in sea level. Climate changes can cause glaciers and ice caps to melt and reform causing sea levels to rise and fall on time scales of hundreds to thousands of years. Longer-term climate variations related to variations in the orbit of the Earth around the Sun can lengthen the timescale of sea level changes related to climate change to hundreds of thousands of years for individual cycles. Plate tectonics also influences sea level changes, but on much longer timescales than climate variations. If the process of seafloor spreading and submarine volcanism becomes accelerated in any geologic time period, the volume of material that makes up the mid-ocean ridge system will be larger, and this extra volume of elevated seafloor will displace an equal amount of seawater and raise sea levels. This process typically operates with time variations on the order of tens of millions of years. An even longer-term variation in sea levels is caused by the motions and collisions of continents in supercontinent cycles. When continents collide, large amounts of continental material are uplifted above sea level, effectively taking this material out of the oceans, making the ocean basins bigger and lowering sea levels. When continents rift apart, the opposite happens—more material is added to the ocean basins, and sea levels rise on the continents. These slow tectonic variations can change sea levels on timescales of tens to hundreds of millions of years.

Rising sea levels cause the shoreline to move landward, whereas a sea level fall causes the shoreline to move oceanward. With the present sea level rise, coastal cliffs are eroding, barrier islands are migrating (or being submerged if they were heavily protected from erosion), beaches are moving landward, and estuaries are being flooded by the sea. At some point in the not too distant future, low-lying coastal cities will be flooded under several feet of water, and eventually the water could be hundreds of feet deep. Cities including New Orleans, Miami, New York, Washington, Houston, London, Shanghai, Tokyo, and Cairo will be inundated, and the world's nations need to begin to plan how to handle this inevitable geologic hazard.

About 70 percent of the world's sandy beaches are being eroded. The reasons for this erosion include rising sea levels, increased storminess, decrease in sediment transport to beaches from the damming of rivers, and perhaps shifts in global climate belts. Construction of seawalls to reduce erosion of coastal cliffs also causes a decreased supply of sand to replenish the beach, so also increases beach retreat. Pumping of ground water from coastal *aquifers* also results in coastal erosion, because pumping causes the surface to subside, leading to a relative sea-level rise.

When sea level rises, beaches try to maintain their equilibrium profile, and move each beach element landward. A sea-level rise of one inch (2.5 cm) is generally equated with a landward shift of beach elements of more than four feet (1.2 m). Most sandy beaches worldwide are retreating landward at rates of 20 inches (50.8 cm)–3 feet (0.91 m) per year, consistent with sea-level rise of an inch every 10 years.

Causes of Changing Sea Levels

The average position of the median sea level may appear to rise or fall with respect to the land surface to an observer on a shoreline, and this is called relative sea-level rise or fall. However, it is difficult for the observer on the local shoreline to know if the height of the water is changing, or if the height of the continent is rising or falling. In many places plate tectonics causes areas of the crust to rise slowly out of the sea, or sink gradually downwards below sea level, while the water level is actually staying at the same height. The weight of glaciers or sedimentary deposits can also cause local shorelines to sink, or to rise if the weight is removed. Therefore geologists need a way to differentiate between local changes in relative sea level, and true global sea level changes. This is a difficult problem and is best done by obtaining accurate ages on the time of sea-level rise and fall, and correlating these changes with other places around the world. This has been done through many years of study, and now there is a fairly well established curve of global sea level heights going back in geological time. Local or apparent changes in sea level are called apparent sea level, whereas global changes in the height of sea level are called *eustatic sea level changes.*

Short-Term Climate Changes

Minor changes in sea level of up to about a foot (30 cm) happen in many places in yearly seasonal cycles. Many of these are caused by changes in the wind patterns, as the Sun alternately heats different belts of the ocean, and the winds blow water from one side of the ocean to the other. When water is heated in the summer months it also expands slightly, accounting for sea level changes of an inch (2.5 cm) or so. Thermal expansion associated with global warming may raise sea levels about 12 inches (30 cm) by 2050, and 20 inches (50.8 cm) by 2100. Seasonal development of regional high and low pressure systems that characterize some areas also change sea levels on short timescales. High pressure areas, such as the Bermuda high that often develops over the central Atlantic in the summer, lower local sea levels because the high atmospheric pressure (weight) pushes sea levels lower than in other times.

Other climate phenomena change sea levels more dramatically. For instance, the irregular *El Niño* event, where changes in atmospheric heating cause a warm current to move from the western Pacific, to the eastern Pacific, can raise sea levels off the coast of Peru (and sometimes as far north as California) by up to two feet (0.61 m), enough to cause enhanced erosion, landslides, and cause considerable damage to the

EL NIÑO, LA NIÑA, AND THE SOUTHERN OSCILLATION

El-Niño–Southern Oscillation is the name given to one of the better-known variations in global atmospheric circulation patterns. Global oceanic and atmospheric circulation patterns undergo frequent shifts that affect large parts of the globe. It is now understood that fluctuations in global circulation can account for natural disasters including the Dust Bowl days of the 1930s in the midwestern United States, and many coastal disasters in southwestern South America. Similar global climate fluctuations may explain the drought, famine, and desertification of parts of the Sahel, and the great famines of Ethiopia and Sudan in the 1970s and 1980s.

The air circulation phenomenon known as the El-Niño–Southern Oscillation has profound influences on the development of drought conditions and desertification of stressed lands. Large-scale atmospheric circulation cells migrate north and south with summer and winter, shifting the locations of the most intense heating. There are several zonal oceanic-atmospheric feedback systems that influence global climate, but the most influential is that of the Australasian system. In normal Northern Hemisphere summers the location of the most intense heating in Australasia shifts from equatorial regions to the Indian subcontinent along with the start of the Indian monsoon. Air is drawn onto the Indian subcontinent, where it rises and moves outward to Africa and the central Pacific. In Northern Hemisphere winters, the location of this intense heating shifts to Indonesia and Australia, where an intense low-pressure system develops over this mainly maritime region. Air is sucked in and moves upward and flows back out at tropospheric levels to the east Pacific. High pressure develops off the coast of Peru in both situations, because cold upwelling water off the coast here causes the air to cool, inducing atmospheric downwelling. The pressure gradient set up causes easterly trade winds to blow from the coast of Peru across the Pacific to the region of heating, causing warm water to pile up in the Coral Sea off the northeast coast of Australia. This also causes sea level to be slightly depressed off the coast of Peru, and more cold water upwells from below to replace the lost water. This positive feedback mechanism is rather stable—it enhances the global circulation, as more cold water upwelling off Peru induces more atmospheric downwelling, and more warm water piling up in Indonesia and off the coast of Australia cause atmospheric upwelling in this region.

This stable linked atmospheric and oceanic circulation breaks down and becomes unstable every two to seven years, probably from some inherent chaotic behavior in the system. At these times, the Indonesian-Australian heating center migrates eastward, and the build-up of warm water in the western Pacific is no longer held back by winds blowing westward across the Pacific. This causes the coastal environment in South America. The El Niño phenomenon is described in the sidebar on pages 62–63.

Long-Term Climate Effects

Many changes in the Earth's climate that control relative sea level are caused by variations in the amount of incoming solar energy, which in turn are caused by systematic changes in the way the Earth orbits the Sun. These systematic changes in the amount of incoming solar radiation

elevated warm water mass to collapse and move eastward across the Pacific, where it typically appears off the coast of Peru by the end of December. The El-Niño–Southern Oscillation (ENSO) events occur when this warming is particularly strong, with temperatures increasing by 40–43°F (22–24°C) and remaining high for several months. This phenomenon is also associated with a reversal of the atmospheric circulation around the Pacific such that the dry downwelling air is located over Australia and Indonesia, and the warm upwelling air is located over the eastern Pacific and western South America.

The arrival of El Niño is not good news in Peru, since it causes the normally cold upwelling and nutrient rich water to sink to great depths, and the fish either must migrate to better feeding locations or die. The fishing industry collapses at these times, as does the fertilizer industry that relies on the guano normally produced by birds (that eat fish and anchovies) that also die during El Niño events. The normally cold, dry air is replaced with warm, moist air and the normally dry or desert regions of coastal Peru receive torrential rains with associated floods, landslides, death, and destruction. Shoreline erosion is accelerated in El Niño events, because the warm water mass that moved in from across the Pacific raises sea levels by 4–25 inches (10–60 cm), enough to cause significant damage.

The end of ENSO events also lead to abnormal conditions, in that they seem to turn on the "normal" type of circulation in a much stronger way than is normal. The cold upwelling water returns off Peru with such a ferocity that it may move northward, flooding a 1–2° band around the equator in the central Pacific ocean with water that is as cold as 68°F (20°C). This phenomenon is known as La Niña ("the girl" in Spanish).

The alternation between ENSO, La Niña, and normal ocean-atmospheric circulation has profound effects on global climate and the migration of different climate belts on yearly to decadal timescales, and is thought to account for about a third of all the variability in global rainfall. ENSO events may cause flooding in the western Andes and southern California, and a lack of rainfall in other parts of South America including Venezuela, northeastern Brazil, and southern Peru. It may change the climate causing droughts in Africa, Indonesia, India, and Australia, and is thought to have caused the failure of the Indian monsoon to appear in 1899 that resulted in regional famine with the deaths of millions of people. Recently, the seven-year cycle of floods on the Nile has been linked to ENSO events, and famine and desertification in the Sahel, Ethiopia, and Sudan can be attributed to these changes in global circulation as well.

caused by variations in Earth's orbital parameters are known as *Milank-ovitch cycles,* after the Serbian mathematician Milutin Milankovitch who first clearly described these cycles in the 1920s. These changes can affect many Earth systems, causing glaciations, global warming, dramatic sea level changes, and changes in the patterns of climate and sedimentation.

Astronomical effects that influence the amount of incoming solar radiation include minor variations in the path of the Earth in its orbit around the Sun, and the inclination or tilt of its axis causing variations in the amount of solar energy reaching the top of the atmosphere. These variations are thought to be responsible for the advance and retreat of the Northern and Southern Hemisphere ice sheets in the past few million years, and the associated huge sea level changes. In the past 2 million years alone, the Earth has seen the ice sheets advance and retreat approximately 20 times. The climate record as deduced from ice-core records from Greenland and isotopic tracer studies from deep ocean, lake, and cave sediments suggest that the ice builds up gradually over periods of about 100,000 years, then retreats rapidly over a period of decades to a few thousand years. These patterns result from the cumulative effects of different astronomical phenomena.

Several movements are involved in changing the amount of incoming solar radiation. The Earth rotates around the Sun following an elliptical orbit, and the shape of this elliptical orbit is known as its eccentricity. The eccentricity changes cyclically with time with a period of 100,000 years, alternately bringing the Earth closer to and farther from the Sun in summer and winter. This 100,000-year cycle is about the same as the general pattern of glaciers advancing and retreating every 100,000 years in the past 2 million years, suggesting that this is the main cause of variations within the present day ice age.

The Earth's axis is presently tilted by 23.5°north/south away from the orbital plane, and the tilt varies between 21.5°north/south and 24.5°north/south. The tilt changes by plus or minus 1.5°north/south from a tilt of 23°north/south every 41,000 years. When the tilt is greater, there is greater seasonal variation in temperature.

Wobble of the rotation axis describes a motion much like a top rapidly spinning and rotating with a wobbling motion, such that the direction of tilt toward or away from the Sun changes, even though the tilt amount stays the same. This wobbling phenomenon is known as precession of the equinoxes, and it has the effect of placing different hemispheres closest to the Sun in different seasons. Presently the precession of the equinoxes is such that in the Earth is closest to the Sun during the Northern Hemisphere winter. This precession changes with a double cycle, with periodicities of 23,000 years and 19,000 years.

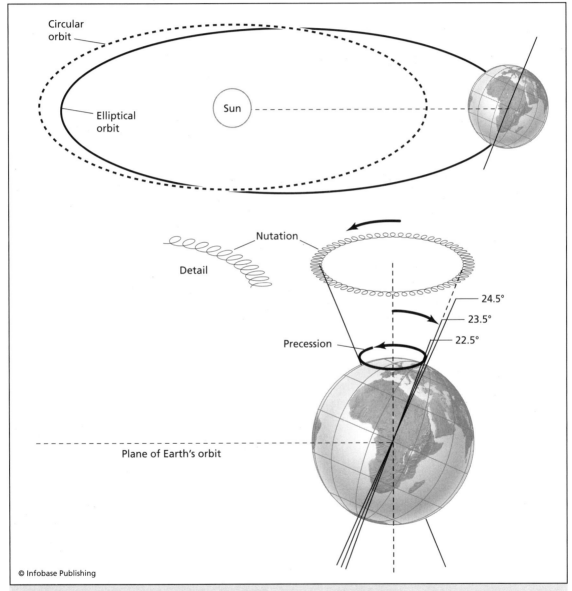

Orbital variations of the Earth cause changes in the amount of incoming solar radiation known as Milankovitch cycles. Shown here are changes in the eccentricity of the orbit that changes with a 100,000-year cycle; changes in the tilt that changes with a 41,000-year cycle, and the precession, that changes with 23,000- and 19,000-year cycles.

Because each of these astronomical factors act on different times-cales, their effects are combined in a more complex cycle. Each of these factors interacts in a complicated way. Using the power of understanding Milankovitch cycles, it is possible to make predictions of where the Earth's climate is heading, whether into a warming or cooling period, and whether sea levels will rise or fall, or if some regions may experience desertification, glaciation, floods, or droughts.

Present data shows that temperatures were about 35.6–37°F (2–3°C) cooler at the height of the glacial advances 12,000 years ago than they are today, and that temperatures may warm an additional 37–39°F (3–4°C) by the year 2100. If this warming occurs as predicted, then large amounts of the glacial ice on Antarctica and Greenland will melt, raising sea levels dramatically. Many scientists predict sea levels will rise at least a foot (0.3 m) by 2100; others predict more. It is likely that the sea-level rise will continue past the year 2100, with at least 16 feet (5 m) over the next few centuries. When this happens, most of the world's large port cities will be partly to largely underwater and world civilizations will have needed to find ways to move huge populations to higher ground. There is a current debate about how much humans are contributing to global warming and the consequent sea-level rise. Most data suggest that human-induced warming is about or slightly less than one degree over the past 100 years, but that warming is superimposed on the longer-term cycles described above. What is not known is how these long-term natural cycles may change. Warming may continue, the natural cycles may reverse, or other sudden catastrophic cooling events may occur, such as a volcanic eruption on the scale of the one in Tambora, Indonesia, in 1815 that lowered global temperatures by about one degree.

Changes in Water/Ice Volume

Global sea levels are currently rising, partly as a result of the melting of the Greenland and Antarctica ice sheets. We are presently in an interglacial stage of an ice age, and sea levels have risen nearly 400 feet (120 m) since the last glacial maximum 20,000 years ago, and about six inches (15 cm) in the past 100 years. The rate of sea-level rise seems to be accelerating, and may presently be as much as an inch (2.5 cm) every 10 years. If all the ice on both ice sheets were to melt, global sea levels would rise by another 230 feet (70 m), inundating most of the world's major cities, and submerging large parts of the continents under shallow seas. The coastal regions of the world are densely populated, and are experiencing rapid population growth. Approximately 100 million people presently live within 3.2 feet (1 m) of the present-day sea level. If sea level were to rise rapidly and significantly, the world would experience an economic and social disaster of a magnitude not yet experienced by the civilized world. Many areas would become permanently flooded or subject to inundation by storms, beach erosion would be accelerated, and water tables would rise.

The Greenland and Antarctic ice sheets have some significant differences that cause them to respond differently to changes in air and water temperatures. The Antarctic ice sheet is about 10 times as large as the Greenland ice sheet, and since it sits on the South Pole, Antarctica dominates its own climate. The surrounding ocean is cold even during summer, and much of Antarctica is a cold desert with low precipitation rates and high evaporation potential. Most meltwater in Antarctica seeps into underlying snow and simply refreezes, with little running off into the sea. Antarctica hosts several large ice shelves fed by glaciers moving at rates of up to a thousand feet per year. Most ice loss in Antarctica is accomplished through calving and basal melting of the ice shelves, at rates of 10–15 inches (25–38 cm) per year.

In contrast, Greenland's climate is influenced by warm North Atlantic currents, and by its proximity to other landmasses. Climate data measured from ice cores taken from the top of the Greenland ice cap show that temperatures have varied significantly in cycles of years to decades. Greenland also experiences significant summer melting and abundant snowfall, has few ice shelves, and its glaciers move quickly at rates of up to miles per year. These fast-moving glaciers are able to drain a large amount of ice from Greenland in relatively short amounts of time.

The Greenland ice sheet is thinning rapidly along its edges, loosing an average of 15–20 feet (4.5–6 m) in the past decade. In addition, tidewater glaciers and the small ice shelves in Greenland are melting an order of magnitude faster than the Antarctic ice sheets, with rates of melting between 25–65 feet (7–20 m) per year, a rate that is apparently increasing. About half of the ice lost from Greenland is through surface melting that runs off into the sea. The other half of ice loss is through calving of outlet glaciers and melting along the tidewater glaciers and ice shelf bases.

These differences between the Greenland and Antarctic ice sheets lead them to play different roles in global sea-level rise. Greenland contributes more to the rapid short-term fluctuations in sea level, responding to short-term changes in climate. In contrast, most of the world's water available for raising sea level is locked up in the slowly changing Antarctic ice sheet. Antarctica contributes more to the gradual, long-term sea-level rise.

Plate Tectonics, Supercontinent Cycles, and Sea Level

Movement of the tectonic plates on Earth causes the semiregular grouping of the planet's landmasses into a single or several large continents that remain stable for a long period of time, then disperse, and eventually come back together as new amalgamated landmasses with a different distribution. This cycle is known as the *supercontinent cycle.* At several times in Earth history, the continents have joined together forming one large supercontinent, with the last supercontinent Pangaea (meaning all land) breaking up approximately 160 million years ago. This process of supercontinent formation and dispersal and reamalgamation seems to be grossly cyclic, perhaps reflecting mantle convection patterns, but also influencing sea level, climate, and biological evolution.

The basic idea of the supercontinent cycle is that continents drift about on the surface until they all collide, stay together, and come to rest relative to the mantle. The continents are only one-half as efficient at conducting heat as oceans, so after the continents are joined together, heat accumulates at their base, causing doming and break-up of the continent. For small continents, heat can flow sideways and not heat up the base of the plate, but for large continents the lateral distance is too great for the heat to be transported sideways. The heat rising from within the Earth therefore breaks up the supercontinent after a heating period of several tens or hundreds of millions of years, the heat then disperses and is transferred to the ocean/atmosphere system, and continents move away until they come back together forming a new supercontinent.

The supercontinent cycle has many effects that greatly affect other Earth systems. First, the break-up of continents causes sudden bursts of heat release, associated with periods of increased, intense magmatism. It also explains some of the large-scale sea level changes, episodes of rapid and widespread orogenesis, episodes of glaciation, and many of the changes in life on Earth.

Sea level has changed by hundreds of meters above and below current levels at many times in Earth history. In fact, sea level is constantly changing in response to a number of different variables, many of them related to plate tectonics. The diversity of fauna on the globe is closely

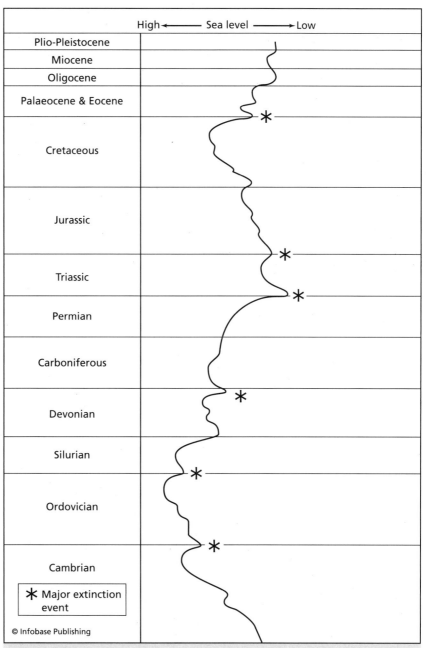

Sea level has risen and fallen dramatically throughout Earth history in response to the supercontinent cycle and plate tectonics. Global sea-level rise and fall must be separated from local subsidence and uplift events along individual coastlines by correlating events between different continents. This global eustatic sea level curve shows the height of the world's oceans after local effects have been removed. Asterisks show the positions of major extinction events.

related to sea levels, with greater diversity during sea level high stands, and lower diversity during sea level lows. For instance, sea level was 1,970 feet (600 m) higher than now during the Ordovician period, and the sea level high stand was associated with a biotic explosion. Sea levels reached a low stand at the end of the Permian period, and this low was associated with a great mass extinction. Sea levels were high again in the Cretaceous.

Changes in Mid-Ocean Ridge Volume

Sea levels may change at different rates and amounts in response to changes in several other Earth systems. Local tectonic effects may mimic sea level changes through regional subsidence or uplift, and these effects must be taken into account and filtered out when trying to deduce ancient, global

This page and opposite: (A) Map of the northeastern Gulf of Mexico coast showing the projected location of the shoreline in 2100, with a presumed sea level height of 3 feet (1 m) higher than present. (B) Detail of the effects of sea-level rise on the New Orleans area, showing how it will be located many miles offshore by 2100, and resting 10–18 feet (3–5.5 m) below sea level except for narrow islands made of the former river levees, that will probably be reworked into a barrier island system.

(eustatic) sea level changes. The global volume of the mid-ocean ridges can change dramatically, either by increasing the total length of ridges, or changing the rate of seafloor spreading. The total length of ridges typically increases during continental break-up, since continents are being rifted apart and some continental rifts can evolve into mid-ocean ridges. Additionally, if seafloor-spreading rates are increased, the amount of young, topographically elevated ridges is increased relative to the slower, older topographically lower ridges that occupy a smaller volume. If the volume of the ridges increases by either mechanism, then a volume of water equal to the increased ridge volume is displaced and sea level rises, inundating the continents. Changes in ridge volume are able to change sea levels positively or negatively by about 985 feet (300 m) from present values, at rates of about 0.4 inches (1 cm) every 1,000 years.

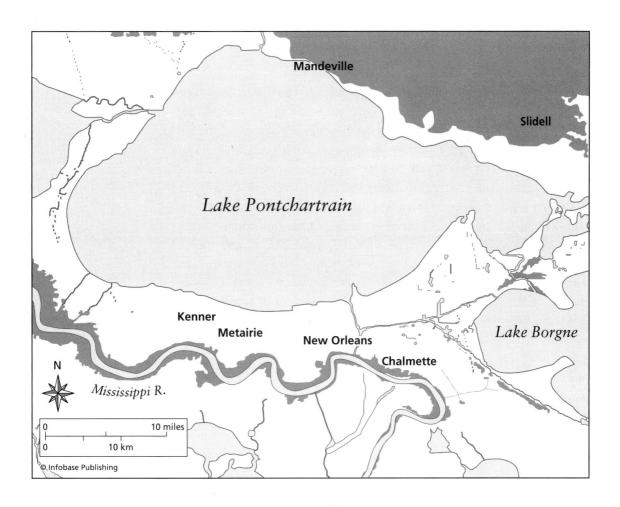

Changes in Continental Area

Continent-continent collisions can lower sea levels by reducing the area of the continents. When continents collide, mountains and plateaus are uplifted, and the amount of material that is taken from below sea level to higher elevations no longer displaces seawater, causing sea levels to drop. The ongoing India-Asia collision has caused sea levels to drop by 33 feet (10 m) in the past 15 million years.

Other things, such as mid-plate volcanism, can also change sea levels. The Hawaiian Islands are hot-spot style mid-plate volcanoes that have been erupted onto the seafloor, displacing an amount of water equal to their volume. Although this effect is not large at present, at some periods in Earth history there were many more *hot spots* (such as in the Cretaceous period), and the effect may have been larger.

The effects of the supercontinent cycle on sea level may be summarized as follows. Continent assembly favors *regression,* whereas continental fragmentation and dispersal favors *transgression.*

Subsidence of Coastal Environments

Natural geologic subsidence is the sinking of land relative to sea level or some other uniform surface. Subsidence may be a gradual barely perceptible process, or it may occur as a catastrophic collapse of the surface. Subsidence occurs naturally along some coastlines, and in areas where groundwater has dissolved cave systems in rocks such as limestone. It may occur on a regional scale, affecting an entire coastline, or it may be local in scale, such as when a sinkhole suddenly opens and collapses in the middle of a neighborhood. Other subsidence events reflect the interaction of humans with the environment, and include ground surface subsidence as a result of mining excavations, groundwater and petroleum extraction, and several other processes. *Compaction* is a related phenomenon, where the pore spaces of a material are gradually reduced, condensing the material and causing the surface to subside. Subsidence and compaction do not typically result in death or even injury, but they do cost Americans alone tens of millions of dollars per year. The main hazard of subsidence and compaction is damage to property. Subsidence can also result in more sinister long-term effects. Many coastal cities are experiencing slow subsidence so that surfaces once above sea level sink to many feet below sea level over hundreds of years. This phenomenon results in putting cities including Venice, New Orleans, and many others below sea level. In the case of New Orleans the subsidence has resulted in the surrounding wetlands to have sunk below sea level, placing the city—now partly below sea level—much closer to the coast than when it was built. Subsidence has therefore contributed greatly to the increased damage to the city from recent hurricanes, and continues to place the city at ever-increasing risk.

Subsidence and compaction directly affect millions of people. Residents of New Orleans live below sea level and are constantly struggling with the consequences of living on a slowly subsiding delta. Coastal residents in the Netherlands have constructed massive dike systems to try to keep the North Sea out of their slowly subsiding land. The city of Venice, Italy, has dealt with subsidence in a uniquely charming way, drawing tourists from around the world. Millions of people live below the high-tide level in Tokyo. The coastline of Texas along the Gulf of Mexico is slowly subsiding, placing residents of Baytown and other Houston suburbs close to sea level and in danger of hurricane-induced storm surges and other more frequent flooding events. In Florida, sinkholes have episodically opened up, swallowing homes and businesses, particularly during times of drought.

The driving force of subsidence is gravity, with the style and amount of subsidence controlled by the physical properties of the soil, *regolith* and bedrock underlying the area that is subsiding. Subsidence does not require a transporting medium, but it is aided by other processes such as groundwater dissolution that can remove mineral material and carry it away in solution, creating underground caverns that are prone to collapse.

Natural subsidence has many causes, all of which may operate in the coastal environment. *Dissolution* of limestone by underground streams and water systems is one of the most common, creating large open spaces that collapse under the influence of gravity. Ground water dissolution results in the formation of sinkholes, large, generally circular depressions caused by collapse of the surface into underground open spaces.

Earthquakes may raise or lower the land suddenly, as in the case of the 1964 Alaskan earthquake during which tens of thousands of square miles suddenly sank or rose three to five feet, causing massive disruption to coastal communities and ecosystems. Earthquake-induced ground shaking can also cause *liquefaction* and compaction of unconsolidated surface sediments, also leading to subsidence. Regional lowering of the land surface by liquefaction and compaction was widespread in the magnitude 6.9 Kobe, Japan, earthquake of 1995.

Volcanic activity can cause subsidence, as when underground magma chambers empty out during an eruption. In this case, subsidence is often the lesser of many hazards that local residents need to fear. Subsidence may also occur on *lava* flows, when lava empties out of tubes or underground chambers. The eruption of Krakatoa in Indonesia in 1883 was associated with rapid collapse of the coastal caldera, and the sea rushed into the exposed magma chamber, generating a huge tsunami that killed 36,000 people in nearby coastal villages.

Some natural subsidence on the regional scale is associated with continental scale tectonic processes. The weight of sediments deposited along continental shelves can cause the entire continental margin to sink causing coastal subsidence and a landward migration of the shoreline. Tectonic processes associated with extension, continental rifting, strike slip faulting, and even collision can cause local or regional subsidence, sometimes at rates of several inches (7–10 cm) per year.

Types of Surface Subsidence and Collapse

Some subsidence occurs because of processes that happen at depths of thousands of feet beneath the surface, and is referred to as deep subsidence. Other subsidence is caused by shallow near-surface processes and is known as shallow subsidence. Tectonic subsidence is a result of the movement of the plates on a lithospheric scale, whereas human-induced

The effects of coastal subsidence and storm damage, showing land loss in marsh around Venice, Louisiana, on October 1, 2005, after Hurricane Rita *(Associated Press)*

subsidence refers to cases where the activities of people, such as extraction of fluids from depth, have resulted in lowering of the land surface.

Compaction-related subsidence may be defined as the slow sinking of the ground surface because of reduced pore space, lowered pore pressure, and other processes that cause the regolith to become more condensed and occupy a smaller volume. Most subsidence and compaction mechanisms are slow and result in gradual sinking of the lands surface, whereas sometimes the process may occur catastrophically, and is known as a collapse.

Human-Induced Subsidence

Several types of human activity can result in the formation of sinkholes or cause other surface subsidence phenomena. Withdrawals of fluids from underground aquifers, depletion of the source of replenishment to these aquifers, and collapse of underground mines can all cause surface subsidence. In addition, vibrations from drilling, construction, or blasting can trigger collapse events, and the extra load of buildings over unknown deep collapse structures can cause them to propagate to the surface, forming a sinkhole. These processes reflect geologic hazards caused by human's interaction with the natural geologic environment.

Groundwater Extraction

The extraction of *groundwater,* oil, gas, or other fluids from underground reservoirs can cause significant subsidence of the land's surface. In some cases the removal of underground water is natural. During times of severe drought, soil moisture may decrease dramatically and drought-resistant plants with deep root systems can draw water from great depths, reaching a hundred feet or more (many tens of meters) in some cases. In most cases, however, subsidence caused by deep fluid extraction is caused by human activity.

This deep subsidence mechanism operates because the fluids that are extracted served to help support the weight of the overlying regolith. The weight of the overlying material places the fluids under significant pressure, known as hydrostatic pressure, which keeps the pressure between individual grains in the regolith at a minimum. This in turns helps prevent the grains from becoming closely packed or compacted. If the fluids are removed, the pressure between individual grains increases and the grains become more closely packed and compacted, occupying less space than before the fluid was extracted. This can cause the surface to subside. A small amount of this subsidence may be temporary, or recoverable, but generally once surface subsidence related to fluid extraction occurs, it is nonrecoverable. When this process occurs on a regional scale the effect can be subsidence of a relatively large area. Subsidence associated with underground fluid extraction is usually gradual but still costs millions of dollars in damage every year in the United States.

The amount of surface subsidence is related to the amount of fluid withdrawn from the ground and also to the compressibility of the layer that the fluid has been removed from. If water is removed from cracks in a solid igneous, metamorphic, or sedimentary rock, then the strength of the rock around the cracks will be great enough to support the overlying material and no surface subsidence is likely to occur. In contrast, if fluids are removed from a compressible layer such as sand, shale, or clay, then significant surface subsidence may result from fluid extraction. Clay and shale have a greater *porosity* and compressibility than sand, so extraction of water from clay rich sediments results in greater subsidence than the same amount of fluid withdrawn from a sandy layer.

One of the most common causes of fluid extraction related subsidence is the overpumping of groundwater from *aquifers.* If many wells are pumping water from the same aquifer, the cones of depression surrounding each well begin to merge, lowering the regional groundwater level. Lowering of the groundwater table can lead to gradual, irreversible subsidence.

Surface subsidence associated with groundwater extraction is a serious problem in many parts of the southwestern United States, and in coastal cities such as New Orleans. Many cities such as Tucson, Phoenix, Los Angeles, Salt Lake City, Las Vegas, and San Diego rely heavily on groundwater pumped from compressible layers in underground aquifers.

The San Joaquin Valley of California offers a dramatic example of the effects of groundwater extraction. Extraction of groundwater for irrigation over a period of 50 years has resulted in nearly 30 feet (9 m) of surface subsidence. Parts of the Tucson Basin in Arizona are presently subsiding at an accelerating rate, and many investigators fear that the increasing rate of subsidence reflects a transition from temporary recoverable subsidence, to a permanent compaction of the water-bearing layers at depth.

The world's most famous subsiding city is Venice, Italy. Venice is sinking at a rate of about one foot per century, and much of the city is below sea level or just above sea level, and prone to floods from storm surges and astronomical high tides in the Adriatic Sea. The city has subsided more than 10 feet since it was founded near sea level. These aqua altas (meaning high-water in Italian) flood streets as far as the famous Piazza San Marco. Venice has been subsiding for a combination of reasons, including compaction of the coastal mud that the city was built on. One of the main causes of the sinking of Venice has been groundwater extraction. Nearly 20,000 groundwater wells pumped water from compressible sediment beneath the city, with the result being the city sank into the empty space created by the withdrawal of water. The Italian government has now built an aqueduct system to bring drinking water to residents, and has closed most of the 20,000 wells. This action has slowed the subsidence of the city, but it is still sinking, and this action may be too little too late to spare Venice from the future effects of storm surges and astronomical high tides.

Mexico City is also plagued with subsidence problems caused by groundwater extraction. Mexico City is built on a several thousand-foot-thick sequence of sedimentary and volcanic rocks, including a large dried lake bed on the surface. Most of the ground water is extracted from the upper 200 feet (61 m) of these sediments. Parts of Mexico City have subsided dramatically, whereas others have not. The northeast part of the city has subsided about 20 feet (6 m). Many of the subsidence patterns in Mexico City can be related to the underlying geology. In places like the northeast part of the city that are underlain by loose compressible sediments, the subsidence has been large. In other places underlaid by volcanic rocks, the subsidence has been minor.

The extraction of oil, natural gas, and other fluids from the Earth also may result in surface subsidence. In the United States, subsidence related to petroleum extraction is a large problem in Texas, Louisiana, and parts of California. One of the worst cases of oil field subsidence is that of Long Beach, California, where the ground surface has subsided 30 feet (9 m) in response to extraction of underground oil. There are approximately 2,000 oil wells in Long Beach, pumping oil from beneath the city. Much of Long Beach's coastal area subsided below sea level, forcing the city to construct a series of dikes to keep the water out. When the subsidence problem was recognized and understood, the city began a program of reinjecting water into the oil field to replace the extracted fluids and to prevent further subsidence. This reinjection program was initiated in 1958, and since then the subsidence has stopped, but the land surface cannot be raised to its former levels.

Pumping of oil from an oil field west of Marina del Ray along the Newport-Ingelwood fault resulted in subsidence beneath the Baldwin Hills Dam and Reservoir, leading to the dam's catastrophic failure on December 14, 1963. Oil extraction from the Inglewood Oil field resulted in a subsidence-related slip on a fault beneath the dam and reservoir, which was enough to initiate a crack in the dam foundation. The crack was quickly expanded by pressure from the water in the reservoir, which led to the dam's catastrophic failure at 3:38 P.M. Sixty-five million gallons of water were suddenly released, destroying dozens of homes, killing five people, and causing $12 million in damage.

Seawater Intrusion in Coastal Aquifers

Encroachment of seawater into drinking and irrigation wells is an increasing problem for many coastal communities around the world. Porous soils and rocks beneath the groundwater table in terrestrial environments are generally saturated with freshwater, whereas porous sediment and rock beneath the oceans is saturated with salt water. In coastal environments there must be a boundary between the fresh groundwater and the salty groundwater. In some cases this is a vertical boundary, whereas in other cases the boundary is inclined with the denser salt water lying beneath the lighter freshwater. In areas where there is complex or layered stratigraphy the boundary may be complex, consisting of many interfingering layers of fresh- and salt water.

In normal equilibrium situations the boundary between the fresh and salty water remains rather stationary. In times of drought the boundary may move landward or upward, and in times of excessive precipitation the boundary may move seaward and downward. As sea levels rise the boundary moves inland and wells that formerly tapped freshwater begin to tap salt water. This is called *seawater intrusion or encroachment.*

Many coastal communities have been highly developed, with many residential neighborhoods, cities, and agricultural users obtaining their water from groundwater wells. When these wells pump more water out of coastal aquifers than is replenished by new rainfall and other inputs to the aquifer the freshwater lens resting over the saltwater lens is depleted. This also causes the salt water to move in to the empty pore spaces to take the place of the freshwater. Eventually, as pumping continues, the freshwater lens becomes so depleted that the wells begin to draw salt water out of the aquifer, and the well becomes effectively useless. This is another way that saltwater intrusion or encroachment can poison groundwater wells. In cases of severe drought the process may be natural, but in most cases seawater intrusion in caused by over-pumping of coastal aquifers, aided by drought conditions.

Many places in the United States have suffered from seawater intrusion. For instance, many east coast communities have lost use of their wells and had to convert to water piped in from distant reservoirs for domestic use. In a more complicated scenario, western Long Island, New York, experienced severe seawater intrusion into its coastal aquifers because of intense overpumping of its aquifers in the late 1800s and early 1900s. Used water that was once returned to the aquifer by septic systems began to be dumped directly into the sea when sewers were installed in the 1950s, with the result that the water table dropped more than 20 feet over a period of 20 years. This drop was accompanied by additional seawater intrusion. The water table began to recover in the 1970s when much of the area converted to using water pumped in from reservoirs in the Catskill Mountains to the north of New York City.

Tectonic Subsidence

Plate tectonics is associated with subsidence of many types and scales, particularly on or near plate boundaries. Plate tectonics is associated with the large-scale vertical motions that uplift entire mountain ranges, drop basins to lower elevations, and form elongate depressions in the Earth's surface, known as rifts, that can be thousands of feet (m) deep. Plate tectonics also causes the broad, flat coastal plains and passive margins to slowly subside relative to sea level, resulting in the sea encroaching slowly onto the continents. More local scale folding and faulting can cause areas of the land surface to rise or sink, although at rates that rarely exceed half an inch (1 cm) per year.

Extensional or *divergent plate boundaries* are naturally associated with subsidence, since these boundaries are places where the crust is being pulled apart, thinning, and sinking relative to sea level. Places where the continental crust has ruptured and is extending are known as continental rifts. In the United States, the Rio Grande rift in New Mexico represents a place where the crust has begun to rupture, and it is subsiding relative to surrounding mountain ranges. In this area, the actual subsidence does not present much of a hazard, since the land is not near the sea, and a large region is subsiding. The net effect is that the valley floor is slightly lower in elevation every year than it was the year before. The rifting and subsidence is sometimes associated with faulting when the basin floor suddenly drops, and the earthquakes are associated with their own sets of hazards. Rifting in the Rio Grande is also associated with the rise of a large body of magma beneath the city of Socorro, New Mexico, and if this magma body has an eruption, it is likely to be catastrophic.

The world's most extensive continental rift province is found in East Africa. An elongate subsiding rift depression extends from Ethiopia and Somalia in the north, south through Kenya, Uganda, Rwanda, Burundi, and Tanzania, then swings back toward the coast through Malawi and Mozambique. The East African rift system contains the oldest hominid fossils, and is also host to areas of rapid land surface subsidence. Earthquakes are common, as are volcanic eruptions such as the catastrophic eruption of Mount Nyiragongo in the Democratic Republic of the Congo in January 2002. Lava flows from Nyiragongo covered large parts of the town of Goma, forcing residents to flee to neighboring Rwanda.

Subsidence in the East African rift system has formed a series of very deep elongate lakes, including Lakes Edward, Albert, Kivu, Malawi, and Tanganyika. These lakes sit on narrow basin floors, bounded on their east and west sides by steep rift escarpments. The shoulders of the rifts slope away from the center of the rift, so sediments carried by streams do not enter the rift, but are carried away from it. This allows the rift lakes to become very deep without being filled by sediments. It also means that additional subsidence can cause parts of the rift floor to subside well below sea level; one example is Lake Abe in the Awash depression in the Afar rift. This lake and several other areas near Djibouti rest hundreds of feet below sea level. These lakes, by virtue of being so deep, become stratified with respect to dissolved oxygen, methane, and other gases. Methane is locally extracted from these lakes for fuel, although periodically the gas concentration in the lower layers becomes so high that the lower layers rise up through the upper layers, overturning the lake's waters, and leading to the hazardous release of gases.

When continental rifts continue to extend and subside, they eventually extend far enough that a young narrow ocean forms in the middle of the rift. An example of where a rift has evolved into such a young ocean is the Red Sea in the Middle East. The borders of the Red Sea are marked by large faults that down drop blocks of crust towards the center of the sea, and the blocks rotate and subside dramatically in this process. Most areas on the margin of the Red Sea are not heavily developed, but some areas, such as Sharm al-Sheikh on the southern tip of the Sinai Peninsula, have large resorts along the coast. These areas are prone to rapid subsidence by faulting, and pose significant risks to the development in this and similar areas.

Transform plate boundaries, where one plate slides past another, can also be sites of hazardous subsidence. The strike slip faults that comprise transform plate boundaries are rarely perfectly straight. Places where the faults bend may be sites of uplift of mountains, or rapid subsidence of narrow elongate basins. The orientation of the bend in the fault system determines whether the bend is associated with contraction and the formation of mountains, or extension, subsidence, and the formation of the elongate basins known as pull-apart basins. Pull-apart basins typically subside quickly, have steep escarpments marked by active faults on at least two sides, and may have volcanic activity. Some of the topographically lowest places on Earth are in pull-apart basins, including the Salton Sea in California, and the Dead Sea along the border between Israel and Jordan. The hazards in pull-apart basins are very much like those in continental rifts. An example of a transform boundary with coastal subsidence and uplift problems is found in southern California along the San Andreas Fault. Many areas south of Los Angeles are characterized by faults that cause sinking along the coast because the faults have an extensional component along them. Further north, near Ventura and Santa Barbara, the San Andreas Fault bends so that there is compression across the fault, and many areas along this segment of the coast are experiencing tectonic uplift instead of subsidence.

Convergent plate boundaries are known for tectonic uplift, although they may also be associated with regional subsidence. When a mountain range is pushed along a fault on top of a plate boundary, the underlying plate may subside rapidly. In most situations, erosion of the overriding mountain range sheds enormous amounts of loose sediment onto the underriding plate, so the land surface does not actually subside, although any particular marker surface will be buried and subside rapidly.

On March 27, 1964, southern Alaska was hit by a massive magnitude 9.2 earthquake that serves as an example of the vertical motions of coastal areas associated with a convergent margin. Ground displacements above the area that slipped were remarkable—much of the Prince William Sound and Kenai Peninsula area moved horizontally almost 65 feet (20 m), and moved upwards by more than 35 feet (11.5 m). Other areas more landward of the uplifted zone subsided by several to 10 feet. Overall, almost 125,000 square miles (200,000 square km) of land saw significant movements upwards, downwards, and laterally during this huge earthquake.

Compaction-Related Subsidence on Deltas and Passive Margins

Subsidence related to compaction and removal of water from sediments deposited on continental margin deltas, in lake beds, and in other wetlands poses a serious problem to residents trying to cope with the hazards of life at sea level in coastal environments. Deltas are especially prone to subsidence because the sediments that are deposited on deltas are very water-rich, and the weight of overlying new sediments compacts existing material, forcing the water out of pore spaces. Deltas are also constructed along continental shelves that are prone to regional-scale tectonic subsidence, and are subject to additional subsidence forced by the weight of the sedimentary burden deposited on the entire margin. Continental margin deltas are rarely more than a few feet above sea level, so are prone to the effects of tides, storm surges, river floods, and other coastal disasters. Any decrease in the sediment supply to keep the land at sea level has serious ramifications, subjecting the area to subsidence below sea level.

Some of the world's thickest sedimentary deposits are formed in deltas on the continental shelves, and these are of considerable economic importance because they also host the world's largest petroleum reserves. The continental shelves are divided into many different sedimentary environments. Many of the sediments transported by rivers are deposited in estuaries, which are semi-enclosed bodies of water near the coast in which freshwater and seawater mix. Near shore sediments deposited in estuaries include thick layers of mud, sand, and silt. Many estuaries are slowly subsiding, and they become filled with thick sedimentary deposits. Deltas are formed where streams and rivers meet the ocean, and drop their loads because of the reduced flow velocity. Deltas are complex sedimentary systems, with coarse stream channels, fine-grained interchannel sediments, and a gradation seaward to deep-water deposits of silt and mud.

All of the sediments deposited in the coastal environments tend to be water rich when deposited, and thus subject to water loss and compaction. Subsidence poses the greatest hazard on deltas, since these sediments tend to be thickest of all deposited on continental shelves. They are typically fine-grained mud and shale that suffer the greatest water loss and compaction. Unfortunately, deltas are also the sites of some of the world's largest cities, since they offer great river ports. New Orleans, Shanghai, and many other major cities have been built on delta deposits, and have subsided 10 or more feet (several m) since they were first

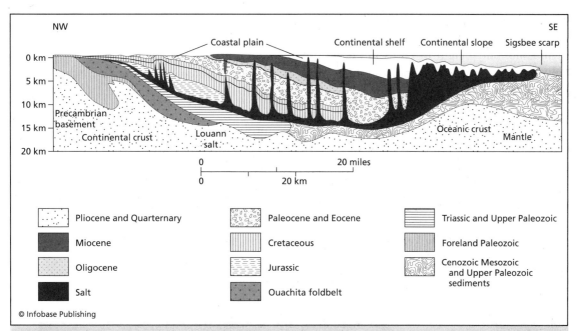

Generalized north-south cross section of the Gulf of Mexico through the Mississippi Delta. The long-term tectonic subsidence of the region can be appreciated by considering how the Upper Paleozoic (~ 250 Ma) sedimentary layers are now 9 miles (15 km) below the surface of the coastal plain near New Orleans, the Jurassic (~200–150 Ma) sedimentary layers are about 6–9 miles (10–15 km) below the surface, the Cretaceous (~140–65 Ma) layers are 6–9 miles (10–15 km) below the surface, the Paleocene to Eocene are 3–6 miles (5–10 km) deep, the Oligocene (34–24 Ma) layers are 2–3 miles (3–5 km) deep, the Miocene (24–5 Ma) is 1–3 miles (2–3 km) deep, and the Pliocene to Quaternary (5 Ma to present) covers the surface. The region has thus been sinking at an average rate of nearly 200 feet (60 m) every million years for the past 250 million years.

built. Many other cities built on these very compactable shelf sediments are also experiencing dangerous amounts of subsidence. What are the consequences of this subsidence for people who live in these cities, and how will they be affected by increased rates of subsidence caused by damming of rivers that trap replenishing sediments upstream? How will these cities fare with current sea-level rise, estimated to be occurring currently at a rate of an inch (2.5 cm) every 10 years, with more than six inches (15 cm) of rise in the past century? Whatever the response, it will be costly. Some urban and government planners estimate that protecting the populace from sea-level rise on subsiding coasts will be the costliest endeavor ever undertaken by humans.

What is the fate of these and other coastal cities that are plagued with natural and human-induced subsidence in a time of global sea-level rise? The natural subsidence in these cities is accelerated by human activities. First of all, construction of tall, heavy buildings on loose, compactable water-rich sediments forces water out of the pore spaces of the sediment underlying each building, causing that building to subside. The weight of cities has a cumulative effect, and big cities built on deltas and other compactable sediment cause a regional flow of water out of underlying sediments, leading to subsidence of the city as a whole.

New Orleans has one of the worst subsidence problems of coastal cities in the United States. Its rate and total amount of subsidence are not the highest but since nearly half of the city is at or below sea level, any additional subsidence will put the city dangerously far below sea level. Already, the Mississippi River is higher than downtown streets, and ships float by at the second-story level of buildings. Dikes keep the river at bay, and usually keep storm surges from inundating the city. However, the catastrophes of Hurricanes Katrina and Rita in 2005, of Hurricane Camille in 1969, and other disasters, shows that the levees can

Subsidence Statistics for the 10 Worst-Case Coastal Cities			
CITY	MAXIMUM SUBSIDENCE Feet (m)	AREA AFFECTED Square miles (km²)	TECTONIC ENVIRONMENT
Los Angeles (Long Beach)	29.5 (9.0)	20 (50)	Oilfield subsidence
Tokyo	14.8 (4.5)	1,170 (3,000)	Delta
San Jose	12.8 (3.9)	312 (800)	Delta
Osaka	9.8 (3.0)	195 (500)	Delta
Houston	9 (2.7)	4,720 (12,100)	Oilfield and coastal marsh
Shanghai	8.6 (2.63)	47 (121)	Delta
Niigata	8.2 (2.5)	3,237 (8,300)	Delta
Nagoya	7.8 (2.37)	507 (1,300)	Delta
New Orleans	6.6 (2.0)	68 (175)	Delta
Taipei	6.2 (1.9)	51 (130)	Delta

Ruins in Cameron, Gulf coast of Louisiana, on October 1, 2005, after nearby towns were decimated by Hurricanes Katrina and Rita. Rapid coastal subsidence has lowered the land surface and levees in this region, allowing the storm surge to inundate coastal regions like this, causing widespread destruction. *(Getty Images)*

not be trusted to hold. Additional subsidence will make these measures unpractical, and lead to greater disasters than Hurricane Katrina. New Orleans, Houston, and other coastal cities have been accelerating their own sinking by withdrawing ground water and oil from compactable sediments beneath the cities. They are literally pulling the ground out from under their own feet.

The combined effects of natural and human-induced subsidence, plus global sea-level rise, has resulted in increased urban flooding of many cities, and greater destruction during storms. Storm barriers have been built in some cases, but this is only the beginning. Thousands of miles of barriers will need to be built to protect these cities unless billions of people are willing to relocate to inland areas, an unlikely prospect.

What can be done to reduce the risks from coastal subsidence? First, a more intelligent regulation of ground water extraction from coastal aquifers, and oil from coastal regions, must be enforced. If oil is pumped out of an oil reservoir then water should be pumped back in to prevent subsidence. Sea level is rising, partly from natural astronomical effects, and partly from human-induced changes to the atmosphere. It is not too early to start planning for sea-level rises of a few feet (about 1–2 m). Seawalls should be designed and tested before construction on massive scales, and moving many commercial and industrial operations inland to higher ground should be considered.

Conclusion

Sea level is rising presently at a rate of one foot (0.3 m) per century, although this rate seems to be accelerating. This rising sea level will obviously change the coastline dramatically—a one-foot (0.3 m) rise in sea level along a gentle coastal plain can be equated with a 1,000-foot (300-m) landward migration of the shoreline. What will the world look like when sea levels rise significantly? Many of the world's low-lying cities, like New York, New Orleans, Miami, London, Cairo, Tokyo, and most other cities in the world may look like Venice in a hundred or several hundred years. The world's rich farmlands on coastal plains, such as the east coast of the United States, northern Europe, Bangladesh and much of China, will be covered by shallow seas. If sea levels rise more significantly, as they have in the past, then vast parts of the interior plains of North America will be covered by inland seas, and much of the world's climate and vegetation zones will be shifted to different latitudes.

It is clear that governments must begin to plan for how to deal with rising sea levels, yet very little has been done so far. It is time that groups of scientists and government planners begin to meet first to understand the magnitude of the problem, then to study and recommend which tactics to initiate to mitigate the effects of rising sea levels. Can massive dikes and sea walls be built? Will our cities look like Venice, with abandoned lower levels, submerged subways, and boats in the street? These scenes will probably not become reality for a long time, but these events are inevitable on geological time scales.

4

Examples of Coastal Hazards and Disasters (1900–2007)

Coastal hazards cost billions of dollars each year in the United States, and when a coastal disaster strikes, a single event such as typical hurricane can cost tens of billions of dollars, or roughly the same amount that the Persian Gulf War cost the United States and its allies combined. Estimates suggest that Hurricane Katrina did about $125–200 billion in damage to the Gulf Coast. However, three years after the disaster, cleanup is no where near complete, and it is estimated that the recovery will cost the United States taxpayers $200 billion to $1 trillion before the time the next hurricane strikes. Coastal disasters also take their toll in lives, with thousands of lives lost in a typical year of hurricanes and coastal disasters. In some years, the toll is astronomical, such as when severe typhoons hit Bangladesh, claiming hundreds of thousands of lives. In the 20th century, approximately 2 million people were killed in hurricanes. In 2004, a tsunami swept through the Indian Ocean, killing more than a quarter million people. Loss of life in hurricanes has been gradually decreasing with better forecasting, whereas at the same time the cost of physical damages to the coastal infrastructure has increased because of the growing population and use of the coastal region. The tables below list the worst coastal disasters, in terms of cost and loss of life.

Coastal hazards are studied by a large number of organizations, including those from the government, university, private, and industry sectors. Several U.S. government agencies help forecast, manage and mitigate coastal disasters. Included are NOAA, the National Oceanographic and Atmospheric Administration, who are responsible for long-range forecasts and short-term prediction of storm paths. NOAA's mission is to conserve and wisely manage the nation's coastal and marine resources. The U.S. Geological Survey and Federal Emergency Management Agency (FEMA) study coastal hazards and make contingency plans on how to deal with specific anticipated hazards and catastrophes. The U.S. Geological Survey performs scientific surveys of the coastal environment, and prepares maps and reports about coastal hazards, and works with other government agencies to help civic authorities know how to deal with coastal hazards and disasters. FEMA deals with emergency management and preparation, and issues warnings and evacuation orders when coastal storms and disasters appear imminent. The U.S. Army Corps of Engineers performs extensive studies of coastal hazards, and designs and builds structures such as seawalls, groins, and dams in order to try to prevent or reduce the hazards at specific sites. The U.S. Army Corps of Engineers is charged with keeping the nation's waterways navigable, and typically constructs barriers that are designed

The worst coastal disasters, in terms of deaths and destruction		
WHAT, WHERE	**WHEN**	**HOW MANY DEATHS**
Typhoon, Bangladesh	1970	~500,000
Tsunami, Indian Ocean	2004	286,000
Hurricane Gorky, Bangladesh	1991	140,000
Storm flooding, Venezuela	1999	50,000
Typhoon Orissa, India	1999	15,000
Typhoon, Bangladesh	1985	10,000
Typhoon, India	1977	10,000
Hurricane Mitch, Honduras	1998	10,000
Typhoons Thema and Uring, Philippines	1991	6,304
Typhoon Linda, Vietnam	1977	3,840
Hurricane, Reunion	1978	3,200
Hurricane Katrina	2005	1,836 (705 missing)

to reduce beach erosion, cliff erosion, and river and estuarine flooding. Many cities and towns located along the coast commission private studies of coastal hazards, and contract with construction firms to help reduce erosion. The university research sector is very active in coastal studies, with many geologists and other scientists who have research specialties in various aspects of the coastal zone.

Galveston Island Hurricane, Texas, 1900

The deadliest natural disaster to affect the United States was when a Category 4 hurricane hit Galveston Island, Texas on September 8, 1900. Galveston is a low-lying barrier island located south of Houston, and in 1900 served as a wealthy port city. Residents were warned of an approaching hurricane, and many evacuated the island to move to relative safety inland. However, many remained on the island. In the late afternoon the hurricane moved in to Galveston, and the 16-foot

The worst coastal disasters, in terms of costs to insurance companies		
WHAT, WHERE	WHEN	COST IN MILLIONS $USD
Hurricane Katrina, United States	2005	125,000–200,000
Hurricane Andrew, United States	1992	19,068
Typhoon Mireille, Japan	1991	14,122
Winter Storm Daria, Europe	1990	5,882
Hurricane Hugo, United States	1989	7,000
Winter Storm Lothar, Europe	1999	4,500
Oct. 15 Storm, Europe	1987	4,415
Winter Storm Vivian, Europe	1990	4,088
Hurricane Georges, Caribbean United States	1998	3,622
Typhoon Bart, Japan	1999	2,980
Hurricane Floyd, United States and Bahamas	1999	2,360

Map of the United States–Gulf of Mexico coast showing locations of many of the cities prone to coastal disasters, including New Orleans, Houston, Galveston, Brownsville, Mobile, and Miami.

(5-m) storm surge hit at high tide covering the entire island with water. The storm surge undermined all of the islands four bridges, including three railroad bridges, and shredded them into timbers that swept with the other debris through the city. Central barometric pressures were recorded at 27.49 inches (70 cm), (931 mbars). Even the highest point on the island was covered with one foot (0.3 m) of water. Winds of 140 MPH (225 km/hr) destroyed wooden buildings including many ginger-bread Victorian mansions in the south, as well as many of the stronger brick buildings and cathedrals in the east, and strong stone hotels along the beach. Debris from destroyed buildings crashed into other structures, demolishing them and creating a moving mangled mess for residents trapped on the island.

There were eight ships anchored in Galveston Bay when the storm hit, and these were all thrown into a heap on the southeastern side of the island where they were left stranded as the waters receded. All electricity was cut to the island, all evacuation routes destroyed, and nearly every tree on the island was uprooted or snapped off at the base. The storm continued through the night, battering the island and city with 30-foot (9-m) high waves. In the morning, residents who found shelter emerged to see half of the city totally destroyed, and the other half severely damaged. But worst of all, thousands of bodies were strewn everywhere—between 6,000 and 8,000 who died within the first few hours of landfall of the hurricane. There was no way off the island as all boats and bridges were destroyed, so survivors were in danger of disease from the decaying bodies. When help arrived from the mainland, the survivors needed to dispose of the bodies before cholera set in, so they put the decaying corpses on barges, and dumped them at sea. However, the tides and waves soon brought the bodies back, and they eventually had to be burned in giant funeral pyres built from wood from the destroyed city. An additional 2,000 people died on mainland Texas from the drowning rains and high winds as the hurricane moved inland. Galveston was rebuilt, and a seawall was supposed to protect the

The devastation along 19th Street, Galveston, Texas, after the 1900 hurricane *(Library of Congress)*

city—however, in 1915, another hurricane struck Galveston, claiming 275 additional lives.

The Galveston seawall has since been reconstructed, and is higher and stronger, although some forecasters believe that even this seawall will not be able to protect the city from a Category 5 hurricane. The possibility of a surprise storm hitting Galveston again is not so remote, as shown by the surprise tropical storm of early June 2001. Weather forecasters were not successful in predicting the rapid strengthening and movement of this storm, which dumped 23–48 inches (58.4–122 cm) of rain on the Galveston-Houston area, and attacked the seawall and coastal structures with huge waves and 30 MPH (48 km/hr) winds. Twenty-two people died in the area from the surprise storm of 2001. Another "surprise" hurricane, Humberto, struck the region on September 12–13, 2007, strengthening from a tropical storm to a hurricane in a few hours and dumping torrential rains on the region, killing one person.

The 1900 hurricane that destroyed Galveston, Texas, was the deadliest natural disaster to strike the United States. This photo shows Lucas Terrace, under which 51 people lie buried after the 1900 hurricane in Galveston. *(Library of Congress)*

Netherlands Storm Surge, 1953

On the night of January 31 and through February 1, 1953, a huge storm surge inundated parts of the Netherlands, southeastern England, Belgium, France, and Denmark. The storm was responsible for drowning 1,835 people in the Netherlands, 307 in England, while 230 people were lost at sea, and 28 perished in Belgium. About 71,000 homes across the region bordering the North Sea were destroyed or damaged. The storm that caused the disastrous surge of 1953 was among the strongest recorded in the North Sea in the 20th century, generating hurricane force winds, and a storm surge that reached 11 feet (3.4 m) in the Netherlands, and 9.7 feet (2.8 m) in England. Sea heights over 18 feet (5.6 m) above normal were recorded at sea.

The worst hit area was the Netherlands, which has a low-lying coastal plain that merges through a series of islands into the North Sea. The flood completely covered this plain in the north, and most

Damage from the storm surge at Zierikzee, Netherlands, on February 9, 1953 *(Associated Press)*

of the deaths were on the islands of Schouwen-Duiveland and Goeree-Overflakkee. In addition to the human toll, about 30,000 farm animals perished in the Netherlands. The unexpectedly high surge rose 9 feet (3 m) above anything that was anticipated, causing the widespread collapse of dikes that were constructed to keep high tides and storm surges out of the coastal environment. The disaster could have been much worse. As the waters rose, volunteers worked frantically to protect South and North Holland by raising the dikes along the river Ijssel. Nevertheless, the floods began to collapse the dikes along the levee, and in a heroic

A broken dike at the town of Abbenbroek on the island of Putten, Netherlands, February 5, 1953 *(Associated Press)*

RETHINKING COASTAL LIVING

Civilized societies have built villages, cities, and industrial sites near the sea for thousands of years. Coastal settings offer beauty and commercial convenience, but also invite disaster with coastal storms, tsunamis, and rising sea levels. The past few years have witnessed two furious incursions of the sea into heavily populated coastal regions, killing hundreds of thousands of people and causing hundreds of billions of dollars in damage. Coastal communities are experiencing early stages of a new incursion, as global sea levels slowly and inexorably rise, increasing the likelihood of additional, even more devastating disasters. These events demand serious reconsideration of priorities about further developing our fragile and changing coastlines. Most pressing is a scientific reevaluation of the decision to rebuild devastated sub–sea level New Orleans in a place where it is doomed to further, more serious disasters and tremendous loss of life. Placing large, generally poor segments of the population at great risk of death and property loss is socially irresponsible. Reconstruction funds may be better used to relocate large parts of New Orleans' displaced population.

The year 2005 began with clean-up and recovery efforts from the tragic December 26, 2004, earthquake and tsunami that devastated coastal regions of the Indian Ocean. One of the worst natural disasters of the 21st century unfolded following a magnitude 9.0 earthquake off the northern Sumatra coast. Within minutes of the earthquake a 100-foot (30-m) tall mountain of water was ravaging northern Sumatra, sweeping into coastal villages and resort communities with a fury that crushed all in its path, removing buildings, vegetation, and in many cases eroding shoreline areas down to bedrock. Scenes of destruction and devastation rapidly moved up the coast of nearby Indonesia, then across the Indian Ocean to India and Africa. Buildings, vehicles, trees, boats and other debris in the water formed projectiles that smashed into other structures at 30 MPH (50 km/hr), leveling all in its path, and killing nearly a quarter million people.

Areas in the United States at greatest risk for tsunamis are along the Pacific coast, including Hawaii, Alaska, Washington State, Oregon, and California. Although most tsunamis are generated by earthquakes, others are generated by landslides, volcanic eruptions, meteorite impacts, and possibly by gas releases from the deep ocean. Any of these events may happen, at any time, in any of the world's oceans, including the Gulf of Mexico, which is prone to tsunamogenic submarine landslides.

In 2005, Hurricanes Katrina and Rita devastated the Gulf Coast, inundating New Orleans with up to 23 feet (7 m) of water. Large sections of the city are uninhabitable, having been destroyed by floods and subsequent decay by contaminated water and toxic mold. The natural inclination to respond to the disaster is to rebuild the city grander and greater than before. However, this is not the most scientifically sound response, and could lead to even greater human catastrophes and financial loss in the future. New Orleans is located on a coastal delta in a basin that is up to 10 feet (3 m) below sea level, and sinking at rates of 0.5–2 inches (several mm to 5 cm) per year, so that much of the city could be 3–7 feet (1–2 m) further below sea level by the end of the century. As New Orleans continues to sink, tall levees built to keep the Gulf, Mississippi River, and Lake Pontchartrain out of the city have to be repeatedly raised, and the higher they are built the greater the likelihood of failure and catastrophe.

Twenty-foot (6-m) tall flood protection levees built along the Mississippi keep the river level about 12–15 feet (4–5 m) above sea level at New Orleans. If these levees were to be breached, water from the river would quickly fill in the 6–20 foot (2–3 m) deep depression with up to 26 feet (8 m) of water,

(continues)

(continued)

and leave a path of destruction where the torrents of water raged through the city. These levees also channel the sediments that would naturally get deposited on the flood plain and delta far out into the Gulf of Mexico, with the result that the land surface of the delta south of New Orleans has been sinking below sea level at an alarming rate. A total land area the size of Manhattan is disappearing every year, meaning that New Orleans will be directly on the Gulf by the end of the century. Assessments of coastal land loss from Katrina are alarming, and push that estimate forward by years.

The projected setting of the city in 2100 is in a hole up to 16 feet (5 m) below sea level, directly on the hurricane-prone coast, and south of Lake Ponchartrain (by then part of the Gulf). The city will need to be surrounded by 50–100 foot (15–30 m) tall levees that will make the city look like a fish tank submerged off the coast. The levee system will not be able to protect the city from hurricanes any stronger than Katrina. Hurricane storm surges and tsunamis could easily initiate catastrophic collapse of any levee system, resulting in a major disaster. Advocates of rebuilding are suggesting elevating buildings on stilts or platforms, but forget that much of the city will be 10–20 feet (3–6 m) below sea level by 2090, and that storm surges may be 30 feet (10 m) above sea level. A levee failure in this situation would be catastrophic, with a debris-laden 50-foot (15-m) tall wall of water sweeping through the city at 30 MPH (50 km/hr) hitting these buildings-on-stilts with the force of Niagara Falls, resulting in a scene of devastation similar to the Indian Ocean tsunami.

Sea-level rise is rapidly becoming one of the major global hazards that the human race must deal with, since most of the world's population lives near the coast in the reach of the rising waters. The current rate of rise of about an inch (2.5 cm) every 10 years will have enormous consequences. Many of the world's large cities, including New York, Houston, New Orleans, and Washington, D.C., have large areas located within a few feet of sea level. If sea levels rise even three feet (1 m) many of the city streets will be underwater, not to mention basements, subway lines, and other underground facilities. New Orleans will be the first to go under, lying a remarkable 10–18 feet (3–5 m) below projected sea level, on the coast, at the turn of the next century. At this point we should not be rebuilding major coastal cities in deep holes along the sinking, hurricane-prone coast. It is time that governments, planners, and scientists begin to make more sophisticated plans for action during times of rising sea levels. The first step would be to use the reconstruction money for rebuilding New Orleans as a bigger, better, stronger city in a location where it is above sea level, and will last for more than a couple decades, saving the lives and livelihoods of hundreds of thousands of people.

New Orleans is sinking further below sea level every year, and getting closer to the approaching shoreline. Sea level is rising, and more catastrophic hurricanes and floods are certain to occur in the next hundred years. Americans must decide whether to spend hundreds of billions of tax dollars to rebuild a city with historic, but deep and dangerously sinking, emotional roots where it will be destroyed again, or to move the bulk of the city to a safer location before subsidence increases and another disaster strikes. The costs of either decision will be enormous. The latter makes more sense and will eventually be inevitable. Whether we cut our losses now and move, or wait until an unexpected Category 5 super-hurricane makes a direct hit and kills hundreds of thousands of people must be carefully considered. Katrina was a warning. New Orleans is sinking unbearably below sea level, and it is time to move to high and dry ground.

act, the mayor of the town of Nieuwerkerk commandeered a ship (the *Twee Gebroeders*) and steered it into a break in the dike, effectively plugging the hole and preventing a worse disaster.

The floods of 1953 in the Netherlands led to a massive construction project to build the "Delta Works" a huge series of dikes, levees, and gates that has closed off the mouths of the Rhine estuary, effectively protecting the delta and coastal plain of the Netherlands.

Bangladesh, a Recurring Disaster

Bangladesh is a densely populated low-lying country sitting mostly at or near sea level between India and Myanmar. It is a delta environment, built where the Ganges and Brahmaputra Rivers drop their sediment eroded from the Himalaya Mountains. Bangladesh is frequently flooded from high river levels, with up to 20 percent of the low-lying country being under water in any year. It also sits directly in the path of many Bay of Bengal tropical cyclones (another name for a hurricane), and has been hit by seven of the 10 most deadly hurricane disasters in the history of the world.

On November 12–13, 1970, a Category 3 typhoon known as the Bhola cyclone hit Bangladesh with 115 MPH (185 km/hr) winds, and a 23-foot (7-m) high storm surge that struck at the astronomically high tides of a full moon. The result was devastating, with about 500,000 human deaths and half a million farm animals perishing. The death toll is hard to estimate in this rural region, with estimates ranging from 300,000 to 1 million people lost in this one storm alone. Most perished from flooding associated with the storm surge that covered most of the low-lying deltaic islands on the Ganges River. The most severely hit areas were Khulna and Dhaka Provinces, where nearly half the population of 167,000 in the city of Thana were killed by the storm surge. Again in 1990, another cyclone hit the same area, this time with a 20-foot (6.1-m) storm surge and 145 MPH (233 km/hr) winds, killing another 140,000 people and another half-million farm animals. In November 2007, southern Bangladesh was hit by yet another massive cyclone, estimated to have killed another 5,000 to 10,000 people. Cyclone Sidr hit with 150 MPH (240 km/hr) winds and a 20 foot (6 m) storm surge, making it the worst storm in 10 years. Since 1970 Bangladesh has made large efforts to improve storm warnings to local villages, which is probably responsible for saving tens of thousands of lives from the 2007 cyclone.

Why do so many people continue to move to an area that is prone to repeated strikes by tropical cyclones? Bangladesh is an overpopulated country, with a population density 50 times as great as that of farm lands typical of the midwestern United States. Its per capita income is only $200 per year. The delta region of Bangladesh is the most fertile in the country, and farmers can expect to yield three crops of rice per year, making it an attractive place to live despite the risk of perishing in a storm surge. With the continued population explosion in Bangladesh, and the paucity of fertile soils in higher grounds, the delta region will continue to be farmed by millions, and it will continue to be hit by tropical cyclones like the 1970 and 1990 events.

Hurricane Andrew, Florida, 1992

Hurricane Andrew was the most destructive hurricane in United States's history prior to Hurricane Katrina in 2005, causing more than $19 billion in damage in August 1992. Andrew began to form over North Africa

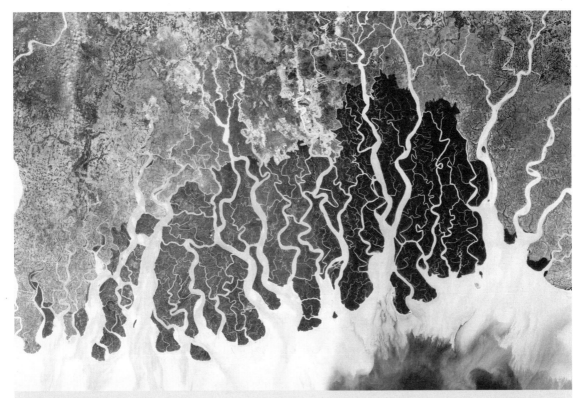

Landsat image of Sundarbans delta at the mouth of the Ganges River, Bangladesh. Note the many islands cut by channels of the Ganges River, many of which get covered by water from storm surges during strong hurricanes. *(NASA image created by Jesse Allen, Earth Observatory, using data obtained from the University of Maryland's Global Land Cover Facility)*

and grew in strength as it was driven across the Atlantic by the trade winds. On August 22, Andrew had grown to hurricane strength, and moved across the Bahamas with 150 MPH (241 km/hr) winds, killing four people. On August 24, Andrew smashed into southern Florida with a nearly 17-foot (5.2-m) high storm surge, steady winds of 145 MPH (233 km/hr) and gusts to 200 MPH (322 km/hr). Andrew's path took it across a part of south Florida that had hundreds of thousands of poorly constructed homes and trailer parks, and hurricane winds caused intense and widespread destruction. Andrew destroyed 80,000 buildings, severely damaged another 55,000 and demolished thousands of cars, signs, and trees. In southern Florida, 33 people died. By August 26 Andrew had traveled across Florida, losing much of its strength, but had moved back into the warm waters of the Gulf of Mexico and regained much of that strength. On August 26 Andrew made landfall again, this time in Louisiana with 120 MPH (193 km/hr) winds, where it killed another 15 people. Andrew's winds stirred up the fish-rich marshes of southern Louisiana, where the muddied waters were agitated so much that the decaying organic material overwhelmed the oxygen-rich surface layers,

Home damage in Florida from Hurricane Andrew, August 24, 1992. This was one of the most destructive hurricanes in United States history, causing extensive damage to many homes and businesses. *(FEMA News photo)*

suffocating millions of fish. Andrew then continued to lose strength, but dumped flooding rains over much of Mississippi.

Hurricane Hugo, South Carolina, 1989

Hurricane Hugo was a powerful Category 5 Hurricane with top winds of 160 MPH (260 km/hr) that devastated parts of the Caribbean, South Carolina, and North Carolina during the September 1989 hurricane season. The storm inflicted $7 billion (1989 dollars) in damage. The storm killed 82 people and left another 56,000 people homeless, making it the most damaging hurricane up until 1989. It was later surpassed by Hurricanes Andrew in 1992 and Hurricane Katrina in 2005.

Satellite radar image of Hurricane Hugo approaching South Carolina, September 22, 1989 *(NASA/Photo Researchers, Inc.)*

Hurricane Hugo formed as a Cape Verde tropical wave off the coast of Africa on September 9, and grew into named Tropical Storm Hugo on September 11th, intensifying to a hurricane on the 13th. The storm further intensified and caused about $3 billion in damage in the northern Caribbean, Puerto Rico, and the Virgin Islands. Hugo then weakened as it moved across the northern Caribbean, but grew back into a massive Category 5 hurricane as it was crossing the warm waters of the Gulf Stream off the coast of South Carolina. The storm made landfall as a powerful Category 4 storm on September 21 at McClellanville, South Carolina, then turned northward to Charleston, South Carolina, as it weakened, finally moving into New England and eastern Canada.

Most damage from Hugo was reported from the barrier islands of Isle of Palms and Sullivan's Island, where wreckages of homes and boats were piled on top of one another and the bridges linking the islands to the mainland were destroyed. Northeast of the eye of the storm, the storm surge hit with a height of 20 feet (6.2 m) destroying many large tracts of old-growth forest. Near landfall, residents who had taken refuge in a school had to climb into the crawl space in the roof of the building to stay above the storm surge waters that had entered the structure. Inland, the estimated 3,000 tornadoes spawned by the storm destroyed enough timber to build a new home for every resident of the state of South Carolina.

When Hurricane Hugo hit the Carolinas in 1989, it inflicted the most damage ever recorded by a hurricane in the United States. The $7 billion in damage has been exceeded five times since then, showing that hurricane damage is becoming costlier as more and more people move into harm's way in the coastal zone. This movement of the population is described in the sidebar on pages 94–95, "Rethinking Coastal Living."

Indian Ocean Tsunami, 2004

Until recently, tsunamis represented an underappreciated coastal hazard. One of the worst coastal disasters of the 21st century unfolded on December 26, 2004, following a magnitude 9.0 earthquake off the coast of northern Sumatra in the Indian Ocean. During this catastrophic earthquake a segment of the seafloor the size of the State of California, lying above the Sumatra *subduction zone* trench, suddenly moved upward and seaward by more than 30 feet (10 m). The sudden displacement of this volume of undersea floor displaced a huge amount of water and generated the most destructive tsunami known in recorded history.

Several minutes after the initial earthquake, the first wave from the tsunami crashed into northern Sumatra as a huge crest of water more than 100 feet (30 m) high, sweeping through coastal villages and tourist resort communities. The wave hit with such force that it crushed everything in its path, removing buildings, vegetation, and in many cases eroding shoreline areas down to bedrock leaving no traces of the previous inhabitants or structures. The destruction and devastation rapidly moved up the coast of nearby Indonesia, where residents and tourists were enjoying a holiday weekend. Firsthand accounts of the catastrophe reveal scenes of horror, where unsuspecting tourists and residents are enjoying beachfront playgrounds, resorts, and villages, and watch as large breaking waves appear off the coast. Many moved toward the shore to watch with interest the high surf, then run in panic as the sea rapidly rises beyond expectations, and walls of water engulf entire beachfronts, rising tens of feet (10 m) above hotel lobbies, and washing through towns with the force of Niagara Falls. In some cases the sea retreated to unprecedented low levels before the waves struck, causing many people to move to the shore to investigate the phenomena—in other cases, the sea waves simply came crashing inland without warning. Buildings, vehicles, trees, boats, and other debris were washed along with the ocean water, forming projectiles that smashed at speeds of up to 30 MPH (50 km/hr) into other structures, leveling all in its path, and killing more than a quarter million people.

The displaced water formed a deep water tsunami that moved at speeds of 500 MPH (800 km/hr) across the Indian Ocean, smashing within an hour into Sri Lanka and southern India, wiping away entire fishing communities and causing additional widespread destruction of the shore environment. South of India are many small islands including the Maldives, the Chagos, and the Seychelles, many of which have maximum elevations of only a few to a few tens of feet (10 m) above normal sea level. As the tsunami approached these islands, many wildlife species and primitive tribal residents fled to the deep forest, perhaps sensing the danger as the sea retreated and the ground trembled with the approaching wall of water. As the tsunami heights were higher than many of the maximum elevations of some of these islands, the forest was able to protect and save many lives in places where the tsunami

caused sea levels to rise with less force than in places where the shoreline geometry caused large breaking waves to crash ashore.

Several hours later, the tsunami reached the shores of Africa and
Madagascar, and though, with distance from the source, its height was
diminished to less than 10 feet (3 m) several hundred people were killed
by the waves and high water. Kenya and Somalia were hit relatively
severely, with harbors experiencing rapid and unpredictable rises and
falls in sea level, and many boats and people were washed out to sea.
Villages in coastal eastern Madagascar, recently devastated by tropical
cyclones, were hit by large waves, washing homes and people into the
sea, and forming new coastal shoreline patterns.

The tsunami traveled around the world, being measured as minor
changes in sea level more than 24 hours later in the north Atlantic and
Pacific. Overall, more than 283,000 people perished in the December
26th Indian Ocean tsunami, though many could perhaps have been
saved if a tsunami warning system had been in place. Tsunami warning
systems have been developed that are capable of saving many lives by
alerting residents of coastal areas that a tsunami is approaching their
location. These systems are most effective for areas located more than
500 miles (800 km), or one hour away from the source region of the
tsunami, but may also prove effective at saving lives in closer areas.
International and local governments have now built a tsunami warning
system for the Indian Ocean in response to the 2004 tsunami disaster.

What Can Be Done to Reduce Coastal Hazards?

Great progress has been made is predicting when and where certain
coastal hazards may become disasters, especially hurricanes. These
advances have been made primarily because of scientists' ability to
monitor the progress of these super storms with satellites and recon-
naissance aircraft. These changes have caused a significant decrease in
the number of deaths from hurricanes during the last century. However,
the population of the United States is continuing to migrate to coastal
regions in record numbers, and the dollar value of property losses has
been steadily increasing. People who build on the coast must come to
realize that their structures are temporary, and society in general should
not be made to bear the costs of rebuilding the structures that individuals knowingly constructed in hazardous zones. Insurance companies,
states, and the federal government should stop insuring and subsidiz-
ing the rebuilding of communities devastated by storms, coastal erosion, and other coastal hazards, and begin to let these areas return to

A front-end loader dumps sand from water's edge to restore dune sheared off by Hurricane Opal, Grayton Beach, Florida, October 24, 1995. *(Associated Press)*

their natural, preconstruction state. Many communities and states have begun to initiate such policies, such as the Cape Cod National Seashore, and the Outer Banks of North Carolina. Since Hurricane Katrina, FEMA, the Army Corps of Engineers, and many insurance companies have been reassessing the risks to coastal environments, and the cost and availability of insurance are starting to change.

In order to better understand which areas are prone to the most severe coastal hazards, the nation needs to continue with a serious program of mapping hazard zones and areas of high risk. This could be carried out effectively by the U.S. Geological Survey and university groups, perhaps working together to complete the work on a national scale. When the country's coasts are better categorized as to where it is relatively safe to build, and where buildings should never be built, then people will be able to enjoy the beauty of the coast in a safer way that will not cost billions of dollars when disaster strikes.

Personal Safety During Coastal Disasters

Most people in the United States will someday experience a hurricane, and will hear warnings on the radio and television of where the approaching storm may hit, how powerful it may be, and instructions about what residents should do to ensure personal safety. The best

A dome home touted as hurricane-proof by Dome Technology in Idaho, is seen here in West Palm Beach, Florida, May 18, 2006. *(Getty Images)*

option for people in a coastal area expected to be hit by a major hurricane is to evacuate. For regions that are difficult to evacuate, it is best to leave early. Experiences from recent hurricanes including Katrina and Rita have shown that monstrous traffic jams can block highways leading away from the coast for days, and a car is not a very safe place to try to ride out a storm in. Take the advice of the authorities, leave early, give up the beach vacation or home and get to higher ground so that it is possible to live to visit the coast again.

Coastal cliffs should be avoided during and after storms and wet periods, as they are most prone to collapse and slumping when the cliff material is saturated in water. Buildings should not be placed near cliff edges, or at their bases.

Other coastal hazards do not usually strike so rapidly. Longshore drift is a slow process, and greater understanding of how the beaches are a dynamic environment will help engineers understand that it is not effective to build groins, seawalls, and other artificial barriers in attempts to slow erosion or divert waves. It is best to leave the beach alone; realizing it is a dynamic complex environment. Changing one thing on a beach will change many others, and it is impossible to isolate and change one characteristic without changing the very nature of the beach.

Conclusion

Low-lying coastal areas in tropical and subtropical climate zones are most prone to being hit by storm surges and hurricanes, inundating the coast with storm surges that can be 20–30 feet (6–9 m) high. Large waves, high winds and tornadoes on top of the elevated sea levels cause major destruction, while most deaths in coastal disasters come from drownings in the storm surge. The country of Bangladesh seems to attract the greatest number of typhoon-related coastal disasters, with repeated events where hundreds of thousands of people have been killed by flooding associated with coastal storms. Low-lying areas in the United States, especially Florida and the Gulf of Mexico coastline, also endure large numbers of hurricanes, which are growing in intensity and frequency. More and more people are moving into coastal areas, putting large segments of the population at risk for injury, death, or property loss. The mass population shift to the coast needs to be reconsidered in the light of the threat from coastal storms, tsunamis, and rising sea level.

5

New Orleans:
The City Most at Risk
for Coastal Disaster
in the United States

The city of New Orleans in southern Louisiana has suffered some of the worst and most often repeated hurricane damage and storm surge-related flooding of any city in the United States. The city reports the highest number of repeat-case flood claims to insurance companies anywhere in the country and, despite hundreds of billions of dollars of attempts to make the city safe, much of it still is at great risk for hurricane-related damage and casualties.

Native American tribes who lived in the area understood the flood risks of the delta plain in the New Orleans area, and preferred to settle along the highlands near the present site of Baton Rouge to the north. South of Baton Rouge, the modern Mississippi delta emerges from between the river bluffs, where every spring the river would overflow the banks and fill the flood plain all the way to the base of the bluffs. Before the levees were built, the spring floods would cover most of the delta except for the natural levees south of Baton Rouge for nearly three months per year. These floods brought many diseases including malaria to early settlers in the early 1700s, and made life on the delta unpleasant if not deadly. After the city site was established on paper by the French by 1725, various trenches, dikes, and water diversion schemes were devised to keep the water out of the town sites, and have always encountered difficulties with the construction. A levee was built around the city from 1718–27, stretching a little over a mile in length (5,400 feet, or 1,646 m) and was 4 feet (1.2 m) high. Early builders noted that the surface 2.5 feet (.75 m) was marked by hard dry mud, but that below that layer the soils were made of soft water-rich mud that could not support structures. Houses came to be built on complex systems of vertical pilings, each sunk about 20 feet (6 m) into the mud, so that the houses are essentially floating on these vertical piers. Many modern homes in New Orleans are still built on slabs on pilings, and the tall modern buildings in downtown are designed so that they float on frictional pilings. As the population of New Orleans grew, many swamps were drained, levees built around the new "land," and the areas were quickly populated. The problem was that the mud in these areas quickly compacted, and these regions sank below sea level. To protect the residents in these subsea level neighborhoods, the levees around the city had to be repeatedly raised and lengthened. However, adding more weight to the levees caused them to sink further in the mud, so they had to be raised again. In addition to the sinking and compaction, the whole region is experiencing tectonic subsidence so that much of the city that is now many feet below sea level was initially built above sea level. As sea level rises, the problem is becoming worse and more dangerous. In the late 1800s the Mississippi River levee commission greatly extended the levee system after a series of floods, and the effort continues until this day. The present-day levee system include some levees more than 50 feet (15 m) tall, and the system extends from the mouth of the Mississippi well past St. Louis, for a total length of 2,203 miles (3,547 km) long.

Large parts of the city of New Orleans now rest several to a dozen feet (1–3 m) below sea level. The city is completely surrounded by dikes and levees to keep the Gulf of Mexico and Mississippi River water out of the city streets and homes. There is limited access to the city, including a long narrow bridge over Lake Ponchartrain. Before Hurricane Katrina struck in 2005, scientists warned that coastal subsidence, land loss, and restricted evacuation routes out of New Orleans have created a dangerous situation where hundreds of thousands of people may become trapped in a city below sea level during a direct hit from a powerful hurricane. Scientists predicted that the levees would break, the city would be flooded, and thousands of people would die (see sidebar on pages 118–119). Few planners listened, and the disaster was realized. Furthermore, the problem is now worse, and it could happen again.

If a hurricane is powerful enough to add flooding rains upriver of New Orleans, the course of the Mississippi could be changed. The

Mississippi has switched courses many times over the past several thousand years, and when that occurs the active part of the delta stops receiving sediment replenishment and it subsides below sea level. Right now, the Mississippi follows a sinuous path past New Orleans and drains into the Gulf of Mexico. Years ago, the Mississippi started to build a new shorter course to the Gulf of Mexico along the Atchafalaya River. The

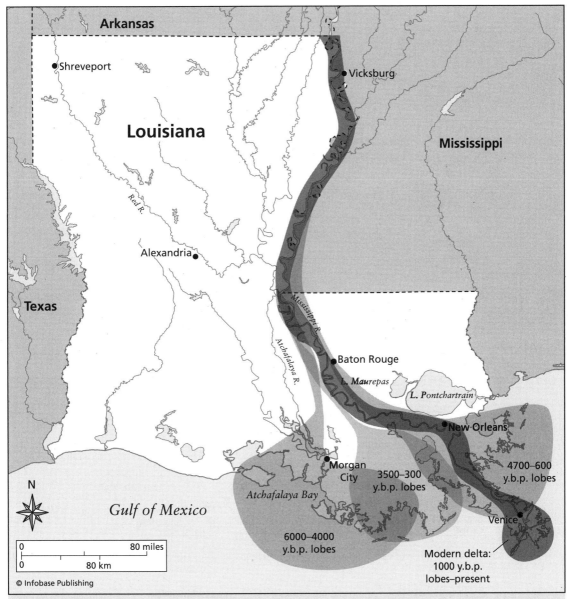

Map of southern Louisiana, New Orleans, and the Atchafalaya River

now be flowing along this shorter, lower energy route if the Army Corps of Engineers had not built a series of dikes and dams to keep the flow in the Mississippi. However, if a hurricane causes a large flood here, the

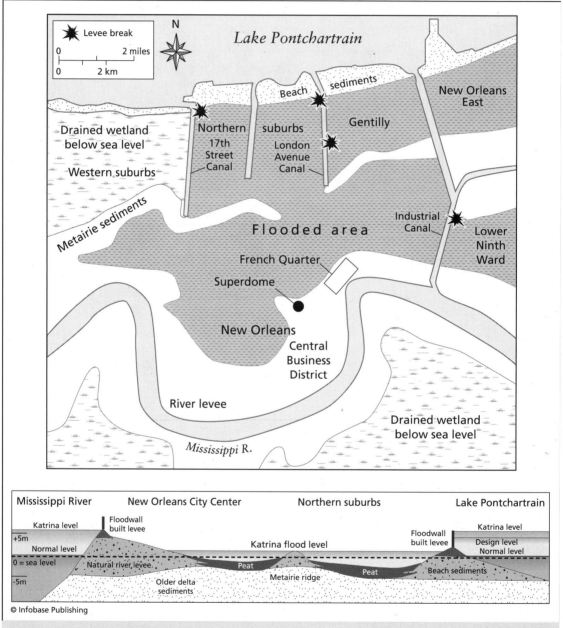

Map of New Orleans showing main flooded (below sea level) and nonflooded areas during Hurricanes Katrina and Rita, and cross section showing the elevations of New Orleans, much of which is below sea level (*Modified after Waltham, 2005*)

here, the engineering works could be breached, and the very course of the river could be changed. This would cause New Orleans and the surrounding part of the delta to subside well below sea level forever.

Louisiana Coastal Subsidence and Disappearing Coastal Marsh

The tragic losses from Hurricane Katrina in 2005 in New Orleans and the Gulf Coast have led many people in the country to inquire about why the Gulf coast is sinking, or subsiding, and what can be done to protect coastal residents. There has been a heated argument between politicians and land developers who claim that the subsidence has stopped, and geologists and engineers who claim the sinking is ongoing and measurable. The argument has led to some confusion in the media and public.

The geological setting of New Orleans makes it a particularly dangerous place because:

- much of the city is below sea level and subsiding rapidly;
- the coastline is retreating toward the mainland as wetlands sink below sea level making urban New Orleans more vulnerable to storm surges;
- sea level is rising and hurricanes are entering a more active and intense cycle;
- the current system of coastal defenses and levees are inadequate to protect lives and property in New Orleans, and;
- if major and costly coastal defenses are not constructed it will be necessary to begin a phased withdrawal or downsizing of New Orleans, by not reinhabiting the most devastated and deepest below sea level parts of the city.

The cause of the subsidence can be best understood as follows. As the weight of deltaic and other sediments is added to the continental shelf/passive margin on the Gulf coast, it presses down and compacts underlying sediments. The weight also causes the entire thickness of the crust and *lithosphere* to sink (tectonic subsidence), much like dirt added to an iceberg would cause it to float lower in the water. As some sediments at great depth, particularly salts and muds, may be able to flow, they tend to move out toward the open Gulf at deep levels, where they can ooze out on the continental slope and form pressure ridges and fold belts. This process is much like sitting on a peanut butter and jelly sandwich, where the bread compacts and the jelly oozes out the sides. Another mechanism by which the weight of the sediments causes subsidence is that gravity and the weight triggers motion on long-lived curved faults. These faults curve toward the open Gulf, and sink slowly downward and outward as material is deposited on them, causing the surface above the faults to sink. Together, these processes all allow the delta and shelf to gradually grow outward and the surface to slowly sink. If sediments are not regularly added to the surface layer, then the surface will subside below sea level. This sediment deprivation can be natural such as when a river switches course, or human-induced such as when a river has levees built on its bank not allowing sediment to overflow its banks.

Approximately one-quarter to one-half of the subsidence of the Gulf coast is tectonic, related to the continuous deep compaction and seaward motion of salts and muds, and motion on deep listric normal faults. Other possible causes of subsidence that together may constitute the other approximately 50 percent of the observed subsidence have received more attention, including compaction of surface sediments, compaction by oxidation of organic soils, loading by buildings, fluid extraction of oil and water, and lack of replenishment of the surface by Mississippi River floods. Some Louisiana scientists, politicians and land developers (in particular, the outspoken biologist D. Boesch) have suggested that the subsidence may have dramatically slowed after the last measurements were made, because some of the surface soils are now compacted. This idea, though it may be partly true, does not adequately consider that the main causes of subsidence are deeper, and that they have been going on for nearly 200 million years.

The component of subsidence caused by relatively recent compaction of near-surface sediments may have slowed recently, because little overbank mud or silt has been deposited since the river has been confined by levees over the past 100 years. Thus, there is little material left to be compacted and the existing mud is already relatively compact. Such an observation does not, however, mean that the underlying deep or tectonic subsidence and retreat of the shoreline has stopped. It is difficult to extrapolate current subsidence rates to the future, as many other factors, including sedimentation and changing conditions, come into play.

Subsidence has many causes, including compaction of the surface layer, motion on seaward dipping curved faults (e.g., two earthquakes in December 2005, and the New Orleans East earthquake of 1987 are related to fault motion that cause subsidence), salt motion towards the

Gulf, deep tectonic compaction, and perhaps fluid extraction and loading by surface structures. The river flood deposits used to keep pace with the subsidence from these various mechanisms, but since the river was constricted by levees more than 100 years ago the flood-muds are channeled out to the deep Gulf and no longer replenish the surface, which is now rapidly disappearing below sea level.

Hurricane History of New Orleans

New Orleans has been leveled or deeply inundated by hurricane-related flood waters about once every 30 years since its founding in 1715, and has been hit directly by 21 hurricanes since that year, meaning one hurricane with at least minor damage hits the city directly every 15 years. The area in southern Louisiana has been struck by approximately 30 major hurricanes in that period, such that somewhere along the Mississippi delta a major hurricane makes landfall about every 10 years, with nearby storms impacting this fragile coastal environment every 2.5 years. With increasing storm frequency and intenstity, plus rising sea levels and sinking land surfaces, it is becoming increasingly dangerous for residents and businesses located along the Louisiana gulf coast.

On September 23–24, 1722, a large hurricane nearly destroyed the newly founded capital city of New Orleans. The storm had 100 MPH (161 km/hr) sustained winds and a storm surge of seven to eight feet (2–2.4 m). Almost every building in the city was destroyed or severely damaged. If city planners has taken this warning when the city only consisted of several dozens of buildings, much damage could have been avoided in the future. A hurricane on August 31, 1794, covered the lower Mississippi delta with a 15–20 foot (4.5–6 m) storm surge, killing 17 British soldiers who were stationed upriver to set up garrisons for local forts, before the storm surge levelled the entire community.

The Great Louisiana Hurricane of 1812 swept ashore southwest of New Orleans on August 19, 1812, with a six-foot (1.8-m) storm surge that moved into Lake Pontchartrain and then completely flooded the city of New Orleans. The storm flattened numerous buildings and destroyed vast amounts of crops, and took an estimated 60 lives. The June 11–12 hurricane of 1815 caused a 7-foot (2-m) storm surge that demolished dozens of homes in the area, and killed numerous herds of cattle. On July 27–28, 1819, the Bay St. Louis Hurricane hit New Orleans with Category 1 strength, battering homes along Lakes Borgne and Pontchartrain, killing about 35 people in the city. Many more perished in neighboring Mississippi where the storm was stronger. In 1837, a hurricane named the Racer's Hurricane spun ashore near the Sabine River on October 6. The rain from the storm forced Lake Pontchartrain over its banks, washing away miles of railroad and driving boats into city buildings. On August 10–11, 1856, the Last Island Hurricane took about 160 lives as it crossed the barrier island of Isle Derniere, demolishing every building on the island. The storm continued to New Orleans where it did vast amounts of damage to city structures. The year 1893 saw the Grand Isle Hurricane move into coastal Louisiana. This storm killed an estimated 2,000 people and remains the deadliest hurricane to hit the state, even surpassing Hurricane Katrina of 2005. The storm hit near the mouth of the Mississippi with Category 4 strength, inundating the population of Grand Isle with a 20–22-foot (6–6.7-m) storm surge and 137 MPH (221 km/hr) winds that removed entire villages and all their traces from the barrier island. Along with the residents, hundreds of vacationers staying in beachfront hotels were killed by this monster storm.

September 20, 1909, witnessed a 14-foot (4.3-m) storm surge across much of southern Louisiana, preceeding a hurricane that battered the entire region, even hitting the state capital of Baton Rouge with 138 MPH (222 km/hr) winds. A Category 4 hurricane spun into coastal Louisiana on September 29, 1915, with a 16-foot (5-m) storm surge that swelled into Lake Pontchartrain and battered New Orleans with hurricane force winds. Almost every lakefront structure in the city was destroyed, and 275 people in the city were killed. On June 16, 1934, a hurricane killed six people as it crossed southwest of New Orleans. September 19, 1947, saw a Category 4 hurricane punching inland south of New Orleans, killing 84 people and causing millions of dollars of damage between New Orleans and Baton Rouge. Starting on September 25, 1956, the region suffered from Hurricane Flossy's movement into New Orleans, damaging many oil drilling structures and causing millions of dollars in damage. On June 27, 1957, Hurricane Audrey washed ashore with a 20 foot (6.1 m) storm surge that inundated much of the delta environment, killing 518 people, destroying 1,900 buildings, and seriously damaging another 19,000. Betsy, a powerful hurricane that became the most costly hurricane to affect Louisiana up until that time, struck on September 7–8, 1965. Betsy killed 61 people and destroyed 25,000 homes in southern Louisiana, leaving 60,000 people homeless. Hurricane Camille, one of the strongest hurricanes to land in United States territory hit the Boudreau Islands southeast of New Orleans as a Category 5 storm on August 17, 1969, with sustained winds of more than 190 MPH (306 km/hr) and a 20–25-foot (6–7.6-m) storm surge before moving into Mississippi. The storm surge moved into Lake Borgne and caused the levees to fail, killing nine people. Many more perished in Mississippi. Hurricane Andrew hit Louisiana on August 26, 1992, with 140 MPH (225 km/hr) winds, causing $5 billion in damage in Louisiana, and $15 billion across the region. On August 29, 2005, Hurricane Katrina hit the Gulf Coast and New Orleans, becoming the costliest natural tragedy in U.S. history. This storm was followed soon on September 24th by Hurricane Rita, which hit New Orleans, coastal Louisiana, and Texas with drenching rains that caused levees that had just been plugged to recollapse, reflooding the city for the second time in a month.

Hurricane Katrina Chronology

Hurricane Katrina formed over the Bahamas on August 23, 2005, and crossed Florida as a moderate Category 1 hurricane. When it entered the warm waters of the Gulf of Mexico it quickly became one of the strongest Atlantic hurricanes on record (sixth strongest ever recorded) reaching Category 5 status with sustained winds of 175 MPH (280 km/hr) with a central pressure of 26.65 inches (67.7 cm; 902 mbar) on August 28 when it was southeast of New Orleans. The storm then lost some of its strength as it doubled in size during an adjustment of the eyewall. The storm made landfall a second time just east of New Orleans at 6:10 A.M. on August 29, as a Category 3 storm with sustained winds of 125 MPH (205 km/hr) that extended outward 120 miles (190 km) from the eye. The storm flooded New Orleans, destroyed much of coastal Mississippi and Louisiana, killed an estimated 1,836 people, and was the deadliest storm since the 1928 Okeechobee Hurricane. In addition to the confirmed deaths, 705 people are listed are permanently missing. The storm continued to move northward, crossing the delta and making a new landfall along the Louisiana/Mississippi border, with essentially the same strength. The storm maintained hurricane strength as it moved inland for more than 150 miles (240 km), where it was downgraded to a tropical depression and eventually moved into eastern Canada. Damage estimates were initially placed at $81.2 billion (2005 dollars), making it the costliest disaster in United States history. Two years after the storm, the federal government had paid more than $113 billion in damage recovery costs (more than $30 billion more than the estimated damage), and many politicians argued that much of the recovery effort funding was being diverted by corruption. By 2007, damage estimates had climbed to between $125–200 billion, and some estimate that these costs will eventually surpass $1 trillion.

Man walking through flooded Terme area of New Orleans after Katrina, August 29, 2005 *(Rick Wilking/Reuters/Landov)*

The detailed chronology of the storms approach to New Orleans, and the government's reaction, is instructive for future evacuation plans. By August 26, many hurricane forecasters were predicting that Katrina might hit New Orleans, causing a massive catastrophe, with the chances of a direct hit raised to 29 percent by August 28. Most of the Gulf Coast infrastructure had been shut down by Sunday, August 28, preparing for the massive storm. The thousands of residents who did not or were not able to evacuate were stranded, as the airport and railways were shut, and roads were becoming quickly impassable. Federal disaster officials were fearing the worst-case scenario might occur. Since 80 percent of New Orleans is below sea level, and the dike/levee system was still under repair from the 1969 damage from Hurricane Camille and continued subsidence, the city was not well-protected—if this were even feasible. FEMA and homeland security models of a storm like Katrina suggested that 10,000–100,000 people could perish

New Orleans resident rescued from roof of home by U.S. Coast Guard, August 30, 2005 *(Associated Press)*

if a storm this size made a direct hit on New Orleans. On August 28, while Katrina was still out in the Gulf of Mexico, it grew to a Category 5 storm, and Mayor Ray Nagin ordered the first ever mandatory evacuation of the city. Many people did not leave, and found shelter in their homes or community shelters, and 26,000 people moved into what were described as desperate conditions in the Louisiana Superdome. Katrina was producing a huge storm surge that was predicted to come ashore with a height of 28 feet (8.5 m), well over the city's maximum levee height of 23 feet (7 m). Actual storm surge heights are uncertain, but were measured at 12–14 feet (4–4.3 m) in southeastern Louisiana.

On August 29th, high waters from the storm surge breached many levees around New Orleans, causing waters to pour into the deep bowl in which the city sits, coming in from Lake Pontchartrain in the north, and along several canals through the city, including the large Industrial Canal. A total area of 90,000 square miles (233,000 km²) were declared federal disaster areas, prompting Homeland Security Secretary Michael Chertoff to describe the aftermath of Hurricane Katrina as "probably the worst catastrophe, or set of catastrophes, in the country's history."

The hurricane brought tornados and drenching rains, with 8–15 inches (20–38 cm) falling, further raising the water level of Lake Pontchartrain and worsening the flooding. The combined effects of the storm surge, wind, and rain blocked most escape routes from the city, knocked out power to nearly a million people, and destroyed the twin-span Interstate 10 (I-10) bridge that formerly connected New Orleans to Slidell, Louisiana. Many areas did not get power back more than two years after the storm, and may be permanently condemned to sink back into the swamps that were formerly drained to make room for suburban development.

The city of New Orleans suffered battering from Category 1 or 2 (74–110 MPH, 118–176 km/hr) hurricane force winds for hours as the storm moved to the northeast. At least 53 different levees were

House destroyed by Katrina, Lower Ninth Ward, New Orleans, still a wreckage two years after the hurricane *(Marc Pagani Photography, 2007, used under license from Shutterstock, Inc.)*

An oil platform ripped from moorings in the Gulf of Mexico by Katrina rests by the shore of Dauphin Island, Alabama, August 30, 2005. (*Associated Press*)

breached during the storm, including the large Mississippi River Gulf Outlet (MR-GO) that broke in more than 20 places, plus the 17th Street Canal Levee, the London Avenue Canal Levee, and the Industrial Canal. Most of New Orleans and surrounding suburban areas were flooded, leaving 80 percent of the area deep underwater. The homes of hundreds of thousands of people were completely destroyed by the flood waters, which carried a soup of toxic chemicals, sewerage, bodies, lost animals and snakes, biting ants, and debris. The winds and storm surge destroyed the Interstate 20 bridge out of the city so the only evacuation routes were to Cresent City, and over the Huey Long Bridge. When the waters receded, many of the buildings that were underwater began to be overrun with toxic mold that posed a new health hazard to any residents who remained.

Downtown buildings reported extensive damage on August 29th. At 7:40 A.M. the Hyatt Regency Hotel reported that most of its windows were blown out, and the winds ripped beds right out of rooms and threw them below into the water-filled streets. The Superdome, which was sheltering thousands of people, suffered extensive damage, with the outer waterproof layer being peeled off, and significant damage to the roof. Hundreds of dead bodies were floating in the streets of New Orleans, and took weeks for emergency officials to recover.

The eye and strongest winds and largest storm surge from Katrina passed over the Gulf coast of Mississippi on August 29, causing massive damage and killing 238 people (with 67 still missing). The storm surge and winds and waves were so powerful that much of the beachfront was completley washed away, and pushed far inland with torn apart bridges, boats, barges, floating casinos, cars, and house debris. The storm's eyewall passed over Bay St. Louis with sustained winds of 120 MPH (195 km/hr). The storm surge was highest to the east of the storm, reaching 27 feet (8.2 m) in height and pushing about 6 miles (10 km) inland in most places but up to 12 miles (20 km) along rivers, bays and estuaries.

This was the highest-documented storm surge in United States history. The Interstate 10 bridge, the Bay St. Louis Bridge (on U.S. Route 90), and the Biloxi—Ocean Springs Bridges collapsed. Hundreds of thousands of trees were snapped from their bases.

Beachfront communities in Mississippi were completely destroyed, with estimates by officials that 90 percent of all structures within a half mile (0.8 km) from the coast were completely destroyed. Long Beach, Gulfport, and Biloxi were nearly devastated, whereas Pascagoula, 75 miles (121 km) east, and the most eastern coastal city in Mississippi, was 90 percent flooded by the storm surge.

Katrina also inflicted considerable damage on eastern communities in Alabama and Florida, parts of which saw a 12–16 foot (3–5 m) storm surge, and battering the coast with washed-up ships and oil rigs, and debris. The storm surge decreased to about 5 feet (1.5 m) along the Florida panhandle, and 1–2 feet (0.3–0.6 m) in central Florida.

WARNINGS BEFORE HURRICANE KATRINA

City, state, and federal officials in Louisiana had ample warning that the city of New Orleans, Louisiana, was at great risk for hurricane damage before Hurricane Katrina hit in 2005. Several geologists had written of the risks and the Federal Emergency Management Agency and Homeland Security made estimates that 10,000 to 100,000 people could perish if a powerful hurricane hit the city. Despite these warnings, city and state officials in New Orleans and Louisiana took little precautionary action, instead focusing their attention on their own political aspirations and business agendas. There was so little cooperation between federal planners and city management that hundreds of school buses sat unused for evacuation, and police were charged with running down looting rings instead of helping stranded residents.

Some of the warnings published before the disaster include the following:

If a fast moving powerful hurricane ever makes a direct hit on New Orleans, it will likely initiate one of the most serious natural disasters this nation has ever seen. Authorities estimate that it will take 72 hours to evacuate the city—even with today's satellites and ability to forecast weather, it is unlikely that an accurate hurricane trajectory could give residents of "the Big Easy" enough time to evacuate. The city will be flooded, dikes will be breached and destroyed, and thousands will perish. Timothy M. Kusky, *Geologic Hazards,* Greenwood Press, 2003.

The Mississippi and other rivers, of course, are not the only threat to Louisiana's lowlands. Every year hurricanes pose a threat from the Gulf of Mexico. . . . New Orleans's defenses would simply crumble if a truly enormous storm lingered over the city for long: a storm the size of, say, Hurricane Ivan, which made landfall along the Gulf coast of Alabama last fall, roughly 150 miles to the east. Even many residents do not realize that New Orleans is on the brink of becoming the next Atlantis, the fabled island

As the storm moved inland, it dropped drenching rains on Louisiana and Georgia, and was associated with numerous tornados. More than 60 tornados were reported from the remnants of Katrina on August 30 and 31 as the storm moved into the eastern United States, then Canada, where it became absorbed by another weather system.

Secondary Effects of Hurricane Katrina

Hurricane Katrina has had profound effects on American policy and thinking about how natural hazards should be dealt with before they become disasters and has led to widespread debate about whether or not New Orleans should be rebuilt. With the repeated destruction of New Orleans by hurricanes every 20–30 years, and the rapid subsidence of the city, many question whether

that, according to Greek legend, sank into the sea. Shea Penland, *Natural History Magazine*, February 2005.

Katrina made landfall at 6:10 A.M. August 29, 2005, as a Category 3 hurricane with sustained winds of 125 MPH (205 km/hr), near Buras Triumph, Louisiana. The levees broke later that afternoon. The rest is history.

After the disaster, officials did little to try to improve their attention to the scientists' warnings, but instead tried to cover these up. Lawsuits were threatened by the governor's office to try to prevent the publication of scientific and news reports. Governor Kathleen Blanco's office initiated campaigns to discredit the warnings of the scientists, hiring their own group of so-called experts to contradict the published results. Congress later commissioned its own scientific study, and concluded that the warnings of the scientists were not only correct, but were understated, and the danger was greater since the city is sinking at twice the rate that was thought, and the levees were already in many places up to two feet (0.7 m) lower than engineers estimated.

The efforts of local officials in the New Orleans disaster were in direct conflict with the best interests of the safety of the residents of the city. Their reassuring statements that all was safe, that the city is not subsiding any more, and had stopped 20 years before (despite approximately 180 million years of history of subsidence), were designed to lure residents back into voting districts and to remain in office and power. Only half of the population returned, but many local politicians were reelected, and continue to try to settle the population into living a dozen feet (3.7 m) below sea level, on an unprotected coast prone to severe hurricanes. Every year that goes by, the region sinks another half-inch to two inches (1–5 cm), while sea levels continue to rise. And every year that goes by, the risk of the Katrina disaster being repeated, perhaps even worse, increases.

the risks and costs of preserving the history and keeping the economic bases in this location is worth the risk. Since Hurricane Katrina, insurance companies have stopped insuring low-lying areas in New Orleans, and this has led to a national reevaluation of which coastal and flood plain areas should be insured and which should not. The U.S. Army Corps of Engineers and FEMA have been working on remapping flood hazards across the nation since the storm, resulting in reclassification of many areas as at-risk for floods. Although this poses hardships on people living in these zones, many people are being allowed to keep their insurance while new homes and businesses are being denied affordable flood insurance.

The economic costs of repairing the damage from Hurricane Katrina in New Orleans and the Gulf Coast are staggering. Two years after the storm, the federal government had already paid more than $130 billion in reconstruction aid, but visits to the region still show widespread scenes of devastation. It must also be remembered that when Katrina hit in 2005, the city of New Orleans was still repairing damage from Hurricane Camille in 1969, more than 35 years before. Therefore it is not surprising that fewer than half the population had returned to New Orleans two years after the storm.

Still not accounted for in the damage estimates to the Gulf region are disruptions to oil flow and supply, disruption of the food supply, damage to the forestry industry, and loss of related industries and jobs across the region. The storm destroyed or damaged 30 oil platforms, and temporarily shut down nine of the nations largest oil refineries. The production was cut to less than a quarter of the normal levels for six months after the storm.

The region's population was dramatically changed by the destruction of tens of thousands of homes in New Orleans. About 300,000 people left New Orleans to settle elsewhere as a result of the storm, leaving the city's population at less than half its pre-storm level. Houston, Texas, gained 35,000 people; Mobile, Alabama, gained 24,000; Baton Rouge, Louisiana, gained 15,000. Many other survivors are distributed across the region and country; for instance, 6,000 Katrina refugees moved into housing in Chicago.

Hurricane Katrina caused dramatic beach erosion, loss of coastal wetlands, and destruction of barrier islands including the loss of the Chandeleur Islands. Coastal subsidence in southern Louisiana results in loss of an amount of land equal to the area of Manhattan every year—in one day, the waves and surge from Katrina removed about

30 years worth of average land loss. Along with this loss, 16 National Wildlife Refuges had to close (or were lost by being swept away by the storm). The impact on the wildlife in the region is severe, but still being evaluated.

Hurricane Rita

Hurricane Rita was the most intense hurricane to ever form in the Gulf of Mexico, and the fourth most intense known from the whole Atlantic Province. The storm formed September 17, 2005, as the Louisiana-Mississippi Gulf Coast region was in the midst of recovering from the floods of Hurricane Katrina. Rita quickly grew to an intense Category 5 storm with winds of 180 MPH (285 km/hr), and struck land as a weakened Category 3 storm near the Louisiana-Texas border on September 20. This storm was particularly painful as it caused the recollapse of the levee system in New Orleans, just as the authorities had managed to pump the city out from the floods of Hurricane Katrina the month before, and the local government planned to reopen the city on September 19. It was also particularly tragic because it hit the regions that many of the evacuees from New Orleans had gone to, and caused the indirect deaths of many caught in traffic jams and other evacuation mishaps.

The largest storm surge associated with Rita was in southwestern Louisiana, where it reached 15–20 feet (4.6–6.1 m). The surge moved up the Industrial Canal, and caused the refailure of the levee system in New Orleans, reflooding the city the day after it was supposed to open to the public after the Katrina disaster. Most damage and deaths from Rita were along the Texas-Louisiana border, and most were indirect, as the result of traffc accidents and similar events. Altogether, 120 people are estimated to have died from Rita, and the region suffered an additional $10 billion in damage.

Rebuilding or Moving New Orleans

Many scientists have warned that the decision to rebuild much of the devastated, below-sea level portions of New Orleans places large segments of the population at great risk of death and property loss and is socially irresponsible. Reconstruction funds could be better used to relocate large parts of New Orleans's displaced population. Many of the former residents of New Orleans seem to agree, as two years after the disaster, only about half of the residents had returned to their former homes.

Hurricanes Katrina and Rita devastated the Gulf Coast, inundating New Orleans with up to 23 feet (7 m) of water, and hitting coastal Mississippi with the largest storm surge (27-feet or 8.2-m tall) recorded in United States history. Today, entire districts of the city are uninhabitable, destroyed by floods and contaminated by putrid water and toxic mold. The natural response to rebuild the city grander and bigger than before could lead to even greater human and financial loss in the future. The U.S. Department of Homeland Security has estimated that a major hurricane hitting New Orleans could kill tens to hundreds of thousands of people.

The city of New Orleans is located on a coastal delta in a basin that is up to 10 feet (3 m) deep and is sinking by one-third to two inches (1–5 cm) per year. The almost 18-foot (5.5-m) levees built around the city to keep out the waters of the Gulf of Mexico on one side, and Lake Pontchartrain on another side, and the Mississippi River on a third side, must repeatedly be raised as the land surface sinks. The higher the levees are built, the greater the likelihood of catastrophe if they are breeched. The levees channel the sediments that would otherwise be deposited on the floodplain and delta far out into the Gulf. As a result, the land surface of the delta south of the city has been sinking below sea level at an alarming rate: A land area the size of Manhattan is disappearing every year. By 2100, geologists expect parts of New Orleans to lie some 18 feet (5.5 m) below sea level and lie directly on the hurricane-prone coast. To save the city, it would have to be surrounded by 50- to 100-foot (15–30-m) levees, making it look like a fish tank submerged off the coast. Still, the levees will not be able to protect the city from the strongest hurricanes.

Advocates of rebuilding the parts of the city that are deepest below sea level need to reconsider the geologic environment of the city. Most of the city will be 10 to 20 feet (3–6 m) below sea level by 2090, and storm surges in the region have historically been 20–30 feet (6–9 m) above sea level. These storm surges, plunging into a 20-foot (6-m) deep hole, would bring a debris-laden 50-foot (15-m) wall of water sweeping through the city at 30 MPH (50 km/hr), hitting buildings, tearing up bridges, and washing away people and most structures in its path. Even without storms, the region faces the danger of continuing sea-level rise. The current rate of rise of an inch (2.5 cm) every 10 years will have enormous consequences for many of the world's large cities, including New Orleans.

It is time for governments, planners, and scientists to incorporate models of sea-level rise in economic development plans. As sea levels continue to rise and cities like New Orleans sink, it is important to protect large populations from hurricane and coastal disasters. Countries such as the United States must decide whether they are willing to spend hundreds of billions of tax dollars to rebuild the city at a location where it is known it will be destroyed again, having suffered catastrophic flooding and hurricane damage about once every 30 years since it was founded, or whether much of the city can eventually be rebuilt in a safer location. New Orleans can serve as an example of what the future may bring as global sea levels rise and hurricanes intensify with global warming.

Conclusion

Coastal Louisiana and New Orleans are built on a subsiding delta that is rapidly sinking below sea level. Efforts to slow the loss are only delaying slightly the geologic inevitability that the coastline is moving inland, and that the delta will eventually regrow elsewhere as part of a natural cycle that has repeated itself many times over many thousands of years. New Orleans and coastal Louisiana have been hit by many strong hurricanes, with about one hit per five years, and with the city suffering catastrophic inundation and losses about every 30 years. Several of these storms have resulted in thousands of deaths, and as more and more people move into low-lying or below-sea level areas on the coast, more and more people are at great risk for death and property loss during major storms. It is time to reconsider the move of the nation's population to the coast, and to resettle displaced people in safer locations.

6

Summary

The coast represents the transition between the ocean, land, and atmosphere, and the specific type of environment developed along any individual coast reflects the complex interaction between these different Earth systems. The coast is one of the most dynamic and changing environments on the planet and the world's population is moving into the coastal zone in record numbers, placing large populations at risk of suffering the consequences of a range of dramatic coastal processes. Understanding the coast is therefore considered to be of great importance for protecting the world's population from future catastrophes such as strikes by major hurricanes on large populations in low-lying areas, and tsunamis that can strike along many coastlines.

Coastal environments are generally different along active convergent tectonic boundaries than along passive margins. Most convergent boundaries have coastlines that are being uplifted, so tend to have rocky shorelines with many coastal cliffs that show rapid erosion. Passive margins are slowly sinking, and tend to have long, sandy beaches, large deltas deposited at the mouths of rivers, and barrier island and inlet complexes located several miles offshore. Coastal bays, estuaries, and marshes of various types may be found along either type of margin, and represent places where seawater and biota mix with freshwater and biota. The beachfront where waves from the ocean meet the land is a high-energy environment where energy from the waves is transferred to the land and is capable of moving parcels of sand half a mile (1 km) or more per day. Many beachfronts and barrier islands are being heavily developed placing people in these communities at risk for catastrophic loss of property and life during coastal storms that move tremendous amounts of sand when the waves, currents, and wind are strongest.

The most important forces that control the evolution and shaping of coastal environments along both active and passive margins include waves, tides, storms, and in geologically recent times, humanity's changes to the shoreline environment. Of these, waves are the most important contributor of energy to the coast and thus are the most important process shaping the shoreline environment. Energy from waves moves sand off the beach during storms and in winter months when the waves are large, and back onto the beach in summer when the waves are smaller. Many waves approach beaches obliquely and gradually cause sand to move along beaches, half a mile (1 km) or more per day in a process called longshore drift. Tides are the periodic rise and fall of the ocean surface caused by the gravitational forces between the Earth, ocean, Moon, and Sun, and cause the alternate submersion and exposure of the intertidal zone along coasts. Tides form very strong currents in the ocean and in breaks between barrier islands known as tidal inlets. The shapes of coastlines can have a strong influence on the character of tides. Funnel-shaped embayments, estuaries, and coves cause tidal waves to become constricted as the water is forced into a progressively smaller area, forcing the wave to become taller, steeper, and in some cases, to form a breaking wave known as a bore that migrates up the bay as the tide floods the bay. Storms such as hurricanes and typhoons can cause some of the most dramatic and rapid changes to the coastal zones, and represent one of the major, most unpredictable hazards to people living along coastlines. Large storms are capable of moving beaches, destroying entire rows of homes, causing great amounts of cliff erosion, and resulting in significant redistribution of sands in dunes and the backbeach environment. Many deaths in hurricanes are associated with drownings in the storm surge, so better prediction of the height and timing of the approach of the storm surge is necessary to warn coastal residents of when they need to evacuate to higher ground. People are modifying the shoreline environment on a massive scale with the construction of new homes, resorts, and structures that attempt to reduce or prevent erosion along the beach. These modifications have been changing the dynamics of the beach in drastic ways, and most often, result in erosion and degradation of the beach. However, the forces of waves, tides, and storms eventually remove many of these structures, often during catastrophic storms that take many lives and now cost hundreds of billions of dollars in damage annually to the coastal environment. The more people that move into harm's way in the dynamic coastal zone, the more these catastrophes are likely to increase.

Global sea level is rising at about one foot per century, but may be accelerating from the effects of global warming. Sea level has risen and fallen by hundreds of feet many times in Earth history, and it is capable of rising quickly as global warming causes a catastrophic melting of the glaciers in Antarctica and Greenland. Rising sea levels cause beaches, barrier islands, and the shoreline to move landward, erode coastal cliffs, and cause estuaries and other fragile coastal environments to be flooded by the sea. At some point in the not too distant future, low-lying coastal cities will be flooded under several feet of water, and eventually the water could be hundreds of feet deep. Cities including New Orleans, New York, Washington, Houston, London, Shanghai, Tokyo, and Cairo will be inundated. The world's nations need to begin to plan how to handle this inevitable geologic hazard.

The coast is the site of some of the most significant natural disasters in history. Recently tsunamis have killed hundreds of thousands of people, and hurricanes annually kill thousands of people and cause hundreds of billions of dollars in damage. Hurricanes repeatedly hit low-lying areas in the path of these monster late-summer storms, with many storms regularly hitting places including Bangladesh, Florida, the United States Gulf Coast, Southeast Asia, and the Caribbean-Mexican coast. Hurricane Katrina in 2005 was the costliest natural disaster in U.S. history, causing hundreds of billions of dollars in damage, killing nearly 2,000 people, and virtually destroying large parts of the city of New Orleans. The Indian Ocean tsunami of 2004 was the deadliest natural disaster of this century, killing more than a quarter million people when a massive wall of water generated by an undersea earthquake off Indonesia swept around the Indian Ocean, washing away villages, resorts, and scouring beaches to bedrock.

Some places have greater risks than others for potentially suffering disasters in the future, as sea levels rise and storms increase in intensity and frequency. New Orleans is the United States' city deemed most at-risk for coastal disasters, as it sits on a coastal delta that is rapidly subsiding below sea level, and much of the city already sits more than 10 feet (3 m) below sea level. It is projected that by the end of the century, New Orleans will be located directly on the hurricane-prone coast of the Gulf of Mexico, sitting in a basin that is up to 18 feet (5.5 m) below sea level. Massive seawalls will need to be constructed if parts of the city are to be preserved from sinking below sea level.

The world needs to consider the effects of rising sea levels on coastal populations on a massive scale. Sea levels are rising at an alarming rate, and more than half of the world's population lives within a day's drive of the coast. As sea levels rise and storms increase in ferocity many of the world's cities will be at greater risk for hurricanes, tsunamis, and other the unfavorable effects of seawater incursions into city limits. It is time to reconsider the global trend of moving toward the coastline, and to recognize the fragility of this environment and let it act as the buffer between the ocean, land, and atmosphere, and to move to higher ground to allow the buffer to respond to rising sea levels and protect the people of the world.

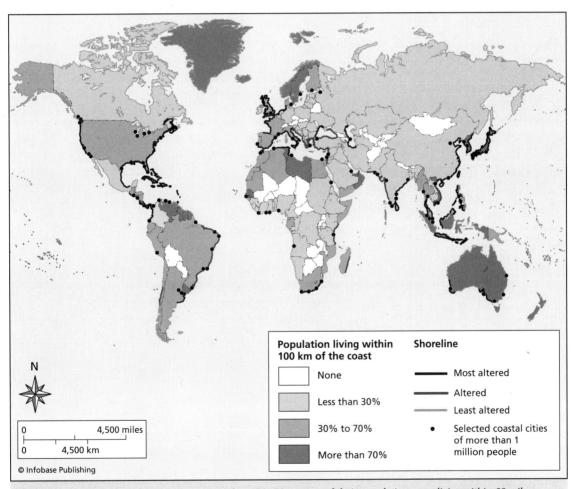

N

0   4,500 miles

0   4,500 km

© Infobase Publishing

Population living within 100 km of the coast

None

Less than 30%

30% to 70%

More than 70%

Shoreline

Most altered

Altered

Least altered

• Selected coastal cities of more than 1 million people

Map of the world showing how many countries have 30–70 percent of their populations now living within 60 miles (100 km) of the coast, and the location of major coastal cities *(United Nations)*

Glossary

accretionary beaches—Wide summer beaches characterized by the movement of sediment from offshore to onshore.

aggrading barriers—Barrier beaches that are growing upward in place as sea levels rise.

amplitude—One-half of the wave height in a wave train.

angle of repose—The steepest angle that a loose material such as sand, gravel, or boulders can be stacked at is known as the angle of repose.

aquifers—Any body of permeable rock or regolith saturated with water through which groundwater moves.

atolls—Atolls and atoll reefs form circular, elliptical, or semicircular shaped islands made of coral reefs that rise from deep water; atolls surround central lagoons, typically with no internal landmass.

backshore—The area extending from a small ridge and change in slope at the top of the foreshore known as a berm, to the next feature (dune, seawall, forest, lagoon) toward the land.

barrier island—Narrow linear mobile strips of sand that are up to about 30–50 feet (10–15 m) above sea level, and typically form chains located a few to tens of miles offshore along many passive margins. They are separated from the mainland by the backbarrier region, which is typically occupied by lagoons, shallow bays, estuaries, or marshes.

barrier spits—Narrow ridges of sand attached to the mainland at one end and terminating in a bay or the open ocean on the other end.

bayhead delta—A delta deposited by a river in a bay or estuary, not in the open ocean.

beach—Accumulations of sediment exposed to wave action along a coastline.

beachface—The side of a coast or barrier island facing the open ocean.

bench—Flat bedrock platform that borders many coastal cliffs, formed by planation by waves.

berm—A small ridge and change in slope at the top of the foreshore.

biosphere—Collection of all organisms on Earth.

bioturbation—The process where organisms burrow and dig into soft sediment and destroy fine-scale layering.

brackish—Water that is mixed in salt content between salty and fresh.

caldera—A roughly circular or elliptical depression, often occupied by a lake, that forms when the rocks above a subterranean magma mass collapse into the magma during a cataclysmic eruption.

centrifugal force—A force related to the spinning of the planet, that acts perpendicular to the axis of rotation of Earth and affects the tides.

chemical weathering—Decomposition of rocks through the alteration of individual mineral grains.

climate change—The phenomena where global temperatures, patterns of precipitation, wind, and ocean currents change in response to human and natural causes.

coastal zone—The region on the land that is influenced in some way by humidity, tides, winds, salinity, or biota from the sea. A more restrictive definition is the area between the highest point that tides influence the land, to the point at which the first breakers form offshore.

compaction—A phenomenon where the pore spaces of a material are gradually reduced, condensing the material and causing the surface to subside.

continental shelf—Generally fairly flat areas on the edges of the continents, underlaid by continental crust and having shallow water are known as continental shelves. Sedimentary deposits on continental shelves include muds, sands, and carbonates.

convergent boundaries—Places where two plates move toward each other, resulting in one plate sliding beneath the other when a dense oceanic plate is involved, or collision and deformation, when continental plates are involved. These types of plate boundaries may have the largest of all earthquakes.

Coriolis force—Arises because the surface of Earth at the equator is rotating through space faster than points on and near the poles. When water or air moves toward the pole, it is moving faster than the new solid ground beneath it, causing objects to be deflected to the right in the Northern Hemisphere, and to the left in the Southern Hemisphere.

cyclone—A tropical storm equivalent to a hurricane, that forms in the Indian Ocean.

debris avalanche—A granular flow moving at very high velocity and covering large distances.

delta—Low flat deposits of alluvium at the mouths of streams and rivers that form broad triangular or irregular shaped areas that extend into bays, oceans, or lakes. They are typically crossed by many distributaries from the main river, and may extend for a considerable distance underwater.

delta front—An extremely sensitive environment located on the seaward edge of the delta. It is strongly affected by waves, tides, changing sea level, and changes to the flux or amount of sediment delivered to the delta front. Many delta fronts have an offshore sandbar known as a distributary mouth bar, or barrier island system, parallel to the coast along the delta front.

delta plain—A coastal extension of the river system comprised of river and overbank sedimentary deposits, in a flat meandering stream type of setting. These environments are at or near (or in some cases below) sea level, and it is essential that the overbank regions receive repeated deposits of muds and silts during flood stages to continuously build up the land surface as the entire delta subsides below sea level by tectonic processes.

depositional coast—A coastline that is dominated by depositional landforms such as deltas or broad carbonate platforms.

dissolution—The process where water reacts chemically with rocks and carries elements away in solution, gradually dissolving the rock. This often results in the formation of caves and other karst features, and may result in underground collapse and sinking of the land.

divergent boundaries—Divergent boundaries or margins are formed when two plates move apart, creating a void that is typically filled by new oceanic crust that wells up to fill the progressively opening hole.

drumlins—Teardrop-shaped accumulations of till that are up to about 150 feet (50 m) in height, and tend to occur in groups of many drumlins. These have a steep side that faces in the direction from which the glacier advanced, and a back side with a more gentle slope. Drumlins are thought to form beneath ice sheets and record the direction of movement of the glacier.

dune—Low windblown mounds of sand or granular material, with variable size and shape depending on sand supply, vegetation, and wind strength.

ebb tide—Outgoing tide.

ecosystem—A collection of the organisms and surrounding physical elements that together are unique to a specific environment.

El Niño—One of the better-known variations in global atmospheric circulation patterns that causes a warm current to move from the western Pacific to the eastern Pacific, and has global consequences in terms of changes in weather patterns.

erosional coast—A coastline that is actively eroding, typically with erosional cliffs or headlands.

estuary—Embayments along the coast that are open to the sea and influenced by tides and waves. Estuaries also have significant freshwater influence derived from river systems that drain into the head of the bay. The fresh and salt water mix within the estuary.

eustatic sea level changes—Sea levels may rise or fall for local reasons, such as tectonic subsidence, or global reasons, such as melting of glaciers. When the sea level change can be shown to be global in scale, it is called eustatic.

extensional plate boundaries—See **divergent plate boundaries**.

fetch—The distance over which the wind blows across an open body of water.

fiords—Glacially carved steep-sided valleys that are open to the sea.

flood tide—Incoming tide.

foredune ridge—A linear ridge of sand that marks the boundary between the beachface and backbeach area.

foreshore—A flat, seaward-sloping surface that grades seaward into the ridge and runnel. The foreshore is also known as the beachface.

glacial erratic—Glacially deposited rock fragments with compositions different from underlying rocks.

glacial marine drift—Sediment deposited on the seafloor from floating ice shelves or bergs, and may include many isolated pebbles or boulders that were initially trapped in glaciers on land, then floated in icebergs that calved off from tidewater glaciers.

glacial moraine—Piles of sand, gravel, and boulders deposited by a glacier.

groin—Walls of rock, concrete, or wood built at right angles to the shoreline that are designed to trap sand from longshore drift, and replenish a beach.

groundwater—All the water contained within spaces in bedrock, soil, and regolith.

high-constructive deltas—Form where the fluvial transport dominates the energy balance on the delta. These deltas dominated by riverine processes are typically elongate, such as the modern delta at the mouth of the Mississippi.

high-destructive deltas—Form where the tidal and wave energy is high and much of the fluvial sediment gets reworked before it is finally deposited. In wave-dominated high-destructive deltas, sediment typically accumulates as arcuate barriers near the mouth of the river. Examples of wave-dominated deltas include the Nile and the Rhone Deltas.

hot spot—An area of unusually active magmatic activity that is not associated with a plate boundary. Hot spots are thought to form above a plume of magma rising from deep in the mantle.

hurricane—A tropical cyclone in which an organized group of thunderstorms rotate about a central low pressure center and have a sustained wind speed of 74 MPH (118 km/hr).

intertidal flat—Flat areas within the tidal range that are sheltered from waves, dominated by mud, devoid of vegetation, and are accumulating sediment. Also called tidal flat.

intertidal zone—The area between the high tide line and the low tide line.

lagoon—A rare class of restricted coastal bay that is separated from the ocean by an efficient barrier that blocks any tidal influx, and that does not have significant freshwater influx from the mainland.

landslide—A general name for any downslope movement of a mass of bedrock, regolith, or a mixture of rock and soil, commonly used to indicate any mass wasting process.

lava—Magma, or molten rock that flows at the surface of Earth.

liquefaction—A process where sudden shaking of certain types of water-saturated sands and muds turns these once-solid sediments into a slurry with a liquidlike consistency.

lithosphere—Rigid outer shell of Earth that is about 75 miles (125 km) thick under continents, and 45 miles (75 km) thick under oceans. The basic theorem of plate tectonics is that the lithosphere of Earth is broken into about twelve large rigid blocks or plates that are all moving relative to one another.

longshore current—The movement of water parallel to the coast along the beachface, caused by the oblique approach of waves.

longshore drift—Gradual transport of sand along a beach, caused by waves washing sand diagonally up the beachface, and gravity pulling the sand back down the beachface perpendicular to the shoreline.

mangal—Dense coastal mangrove-dominated ecosystem.

marine terraces—Wave-cut benches or platforms that are uplifted above sea level, typically occurring in groups at different levels reflecting different stages of uplift.

Milankovitch cycles—Variations in Earth's climate that are caused by variations in the amount of incoming solar energy, induced by changes in Earth's orbital parameters including tilt, eccentricity, and wobble.

moraine—Ridgelike accumulations of glacial drift deposited at the edges of a glacier. Terminal moraines mark the farthest point of travel of a glacier, whereas lateral moraines form along the edges of a glacier.

mudflow—A downslope flow that resembles a debris flow, except it has a higher concentration of water (up to 30 percent), which makes it more fluid, with a consistency ranging from soup to wet concrete. Mudflows often start as a muddy stream in a dry mountain canyon, which as it moves picks up more and more mud and sand, until eventually the front of the stream is a wall of moving mud and rock.

neap tides—Occur during the first and third quarters of the Moon, and are characterized by lower than average tidal ranges.

passive margin—A boundary between continental and oceanic crust that is not a plate boundary, characterized by thick deposits of sedimentary rocks. These margins typically have a flat shallow water shelf, then a steep drop off to deep ocean floor rocks away from the continent.

plate tectonics—A model that describes the process related to the slow motions of more than a dozen rigid plates of solid rock around on the surface of Earth. The plates ride on a deeper layer of partially molten material that is found at depths starting at 60–200 miles (100–320 km) beneath the surface of the continents, and 1–100 miles (1–160 km) beneath the oceans.

porosity—The percentage of total volume of a body that consists of open spaces.

prograding barriers—Barrier islands that are building themselves seaward with time, generally through a large sediment supply.

recurved spit—A sand spit that has ridges of sand that curve around the end of the spit that terminates in the sea, reflecting its growth.

reef—Wave-resistant framework-supported carbonate or organic mounds generally built by carbonate secreting organisms; in some usages the term may be used for any shallow ridge of rock lying near the surface of the water.

regolith—The outer surface layer of Earth, consisting of a mixture of soil, organic material, and partially weathered bedrock.

regression—Retreat of the sea from the shoreline, caused by eustatic sea level fall or local effects.

retrograding barriers—Barrier islands that are moving onshore with time.

ridge and runnel—The most seaward part of the beach, characterized by a small sandbar called a ridge, and a flat-bottom trough called the runnel, and is typically less than 30 feet (10 m) wide.

rip current—A strong current that moves perpendicular away from the shore, typically localized by the presence of a jetty, seafloor topography, or other obstacle. Rip currents are dangerous as they can carry swimmers far out to sea.

rockfall—Free falling of detached bodies of bedrock from a cliff or steep slope.

rockslide—The sudden downslope movement of newly detached masses of bedrock (or debris slides, if the rocks are mixed with other material or regolith).

Saffir-Simpson scale—A hurricane intensity scale that measures the damage potential of a storm, considering such factors as the central barometric pressure, maximum sustained wind speeds, and the potential height of the storm surge.

salt marshes—Coastal wetlands that form on the upper part of the intertidal zone where organic-rich sediments are rarely disturbed by tides, providing a stable environment for grasses to take root. The low marsh area is defined as the part of the marsh that ranges from the beginning of vegetation to the least mean high tide. The high marsh extends from the mean high tide up to the limit of tidal influence.

sea-level rise—The gradual increase in average height of the mean water mark with respect to the land.

sea stacks—Isolated columns of rock left by retreating cliffs, with the most famous being the Twelve Apostles along the southern coast of Australia.

seawater intrusion—The encroachment of seawater into drinking and irrigation wells, generally caused by overpumping of water from groundwater wells along the coast.

sedimentary structures—The organized arrangement of sedimentary particles that form repeating patterns reflecting their origin. Types of sedimentary structures include sedimentary layers, ripples produced by currents moving the sedimentary particles as sets of small waves; megaripples, which are large ripples formed by unusually strong currents; mudcracks, produced by muddy sediments being dried by the sun and shrinking and cracking; and other structures produced by organisms such as burrows from worms, bivalves, and other creatures; trails and footprints.

slumping—A type of mass wasting where a large mass of rock or sediment moves downward and outward along an upward curving fault surface. Slumps may occur undersea or on the land surface.

spit—A low tongue or embankment of land, typically consisting of sand and gravel, that terminates in the open water.

spring tides—Tides that occur near the full and new Moons.

storm beach—Thin strips of sand along a shoreline, formed typically in winter by strong winter storms that move sediment offshore from the beach.

storm surge—A mound of water that moves ahead of and with tropical cyclones and hurricanes, formed by the low pressure in the center of the storm and winds in front of the storm.

subduction zones—Long narrow zones where large plates are being subducted into the mantle; the melting produces a long line of volcanoes above the down-going plate and forms a volcanic arc. Depending on what the overriding plate is made of, this arc may be built on either a continental or on an oceanic plate.

subsidence—The sinking of one surface, such as the land, relative to another surface, such as sea level.

supercontinent cycle—The semiregular grouping of the planet's landmasses into a single or several large continents that remain stable for a long period of time, then disperse, and eventually come back together as new amalgamated landmasses with a different distribution.

swales—The low areas in between dunes.

talus—The entire body of rock waste sloping away from the mountains is known as talus, and the sediment composing it is known as sliderock. This rock debris accumulates at the bases of mountain slopes, deposited there by rock falls, slides, and other down slope movements.

thixotropic—A property of material such as mud where it appears to be fairly rigid when it is held or is still, but when it is shaken or disturbed, it rapidly turns into a fluid.

tidal bore—A breaking wave that migrates up the bay as the tide floods the bay, formed where the shape of the bay constricts the water flow and causes the wave to grow in height as it moves into smaller and smaller areas.

tidal flat—Flat areas along the coast within the tidal range that are sheltered from waves, dominated by mud, devoid of vegetation, and are accumulating sediment.

tidal inlet—Breaks in barrier island systems that allow water, nutrients, organisms, ships, and people easy access and exchange between the high-energy open ocean and the low-energy backbarrier environment consisting of bays, lagoons, tidal marshes, and creeks. Most tidal inlets are within barrier island systems, but others may separate barrier islands from rocky or glacial headlands.

tidal range—The range in sea surface height between the high and low.

tides—The periodic rise and fall of the ocean surface, and alternate submersion and exposure of the intertidal zone along coasts.

till—Glacial drift that was deposited directly by the ice.

tombolo—A spit that connects an offshore island with the mainland.

transform boundaries—Places where two plates slide past each other, such as along the San Andreas Fault in California, and often have large earthquakes, are known as transform boundaries.

transgression—Advance of the sea on the shore, caused by either a eustatic sea-level rise or local effects.

tsunami—A giant harbor or deepwater wave, with long wavelengths, initiated by submarine landslides, earthquakes, volcanic eruptons, or other causes that suddenly displaces large amounts of water. Tsunamis can be much larger than normal waves when they strike the shore, and cause great damage and destruction.

wave base—A depth approximately equal to one-half of the wavelength, where the circular motion induced by the wave begins to feel the sea bottom, which exerts a frictional drag on the wave.

wave fronts—Imaginary lines drawn parallel to the wave crests; the wave moves perpendicular to the wave fronts.

wave height—The vertical distance between troughs and crests of a wave train.

wavelength—The distance between successive crests or trough of a wave train.

wave refraction—A phenomenon that occurs when a straight wave front approaches a shoreline obliquely. The part of the wave front that first feels shallow water (with a depth of less than one-half of the wavelength, known as the wave base) begins to slow down while the rest of the wave continues at its previous velocity. This causes the wave front to bend, or be refracted.

welded barriers—Barrier islands that have grown completely across a bay and sealed the water inside off from the ocean.

Further Reading and Web Sites

BOOKS

Barnes, Jay. *North Carolina's Hurricane History.* Chapel Hill, and London: The University of North Carolina Press, 1995. This book is a readable account of the many hurricanes that have affected North Carolina and the barrier islands of the Outer Banks.

Barras, J., S. Beville, D. Britsch, et al. *Historical and Projected Coastal Louisiana Land Changes: 1978–2050.* USGS Open File Report OFR 03-334, 2050. This government-issued book reports the results of an in-depth analysis of how much land has been and will be lost in southern Louisiana due to coastal subsidence and sea-level rise.

Beatley, Timothy, David J. Brower, and Anna K. A. Schwab. *Introduction to Coastal Management.* Washington, D.C.: Island Press, 1994. This book presents the reader with an overview of how to manage coastal erosion and other issues.

Botkin, D., and E. Keller. *Environmental Science.* Hoboken, N.J.: John Wiley and Sons, 2003. This is an introductory college level book that discusses many issues of environmental sciences.

Bryant, E. A. *Natural Hazards.* Cambridge: Cambridge University Press, 1991. This is a moderately advanced textbook on the science of natural hazards.

Burkett, Virginia R., D. B. Zikoski, and D. A. Hart. "Sea-level rise and subsidence: implications for flooding in New Orleans, Louisiana." 63–70. In *U.S. Geological Survey Subsidence Interest Group Conference, Proceedings for the Technical Meeting,* 63–70. Reston, Va.: US Geological Survey. USGS Water Resources Division, Open File Report Series 03-308, 2003. This is an important research book that presents data that shows that much of New Orleans will be far below sea level by 2090.

Bush, David M., Richard M. T. Webb, José González Liboy, Lisbeth Hyman, William J. Neal. *Living With the Puerto Rico Shoreline.* Durham, N.C. and London: Duke University Press, 1995. This book summarizes the effects of hurricanes and coastal processes on the rocky shoreline and other beaches of Puerto Rico.

Coch, N. K. *Geohazards.* Englewood Cliffs, N.J.: Prentice Hall, 1995. This is a general entry-level college freshman book covering many aspects of geological hazards including hurricanes.

Culliton, Thomas J., Maureen A. Warren, Timothy R. Goodspeed, Davida G. Remer, Carol M. Blackwell, and John McDonough III. *Fifty Years of Population Growth Along the Nation's Coasts, 1960–2010.* Rockville, Md.: National Oceanic and Atmospheric Administration, 1990. This government report shows how half of the nation's population now lives within 60 miles (100 km) of the coast.

Davis, R., and D. Fitzgerald. *Beaches and Coasts.* Malden, Mass.: Blackwell Publishing, 2004. This is a comprehensive, undergraduate to graduate level text on processes and environments on beaches and coasts.

Dean, C. *Against the Tide, The Battle for America's Beaches.* New York: Columbia University Press, 1999. This general reading book discusses problems of construction, erosion, and sea level changes along beaches.

Federal Emergency Management Agency. *Coastal Construction Manual.* Washington, D.C.: FEMA, 1986. This is a manual on how to build seawalls, groins, and protect homes along beaches.

Fisk, H. N. *Geological Investigation of the Atchafalaya Basin and Problems of the Mississippi River Diversion.* Vicksburg, Va.: U.S. Army Corps of Engineers, Mississippi River Commission, 1952. This U.S. government report is about the major water diversion project along the Mississippi/Atchafalaya River junction, trying to keep water flowing mainly down the Mississippi.

Gagliano, S. E. B. Kemp, K. Wicker, and K. Wiltenmouth. *Active Geologic Faults and Land Change in Southeastern Louisiana.* New Orleans, La.: Coastal Environment Inc., Report to the US Army Corps of Engineers, New Orleans District, 2003. This is an important report that documents the role of active faulting in causing much of the land's surface to be sinking in New Orleans and southern Louisiana.

Galloway, W. E., and D. K. Hobday. *Terrigineous Clastic Depositional Systems.* New York: Springer-Verlag, 1983. This is an advanced college book on sedimentary systems on the continents and along the coast.

Godschalk, D. R., D. J. Brower, and T. Beatley. *Catastrophic Coastal Storms: Hazard Mitigation and Development Management.* Durham, N.C. and London: Duke University Press, 1989. This book presents a discussion of how to limit damage when building communities along coastlines.

Hebert, P. J., and G. Taylor. *The Deadliest, Costliest, and Most Destructive U.S. Hurricanes of the Century.* Coral Gables, Fa.: National Hurricane Center, Technical Memorandum, 1988. A review of the worst hurricanes prior to 1987.

Kaufman, W., and O. H. Pilkey Jr. *The Beaches are Moving.* Durham, N.C.: Duke University Press, 1983. This book describes coastal processes including longshore drift, dune erosion, and barrier rollover, and how they present hazards for building along the coast.

King, C. A. M. *Beaches and Coasts.* London: Edward Arnold Publishers, 1961. This is a classic detailed textbook on processes along beaches and coast, and includes discussion of tides, waves, and currents.

Komar, P. D. (ed.). *CRC Handbook of Coastal Processes and Erosion.* Boca Raton, Fla.: CRC Press, 1983. This is a technical handbook of processes involved in coastal erosion.

Kusky, T. M. *Encyclopedia of Earth Science.* New York: Facts On File, 2004. A comprehensive encyclopedia of earth sciences written for college and high school audiences, and the general public.

Leatherman, Stephen P., ed. *Barrier Islands, from the Gulf of St. Lawrence to the Gulf of Mexico.* New York: Academic Press, 1979. This book contains a collection of papers on the morphology and processes on east coast barrier islands.

Longshore, D. *Encyclopedia of Hurricanes, Typhoons, and Cyclones, New Edition.* New York: Facts On File, 2008. A comprehensive encyclopedia of hurricanes written for college and high school audiences, and the general public.

National Research Council. *Drawing Louisiana's New Map: Addressing Land Loss in Coastal Louisiana.* Washington, D.C.: National Academies Press, 2005. This important government publication shows assessments of the astonishing amount of land loss in southern Louisiana, and how much is projected to be lost in the future.

Nordstrom, K. F., N. P. Psuty, and R. W. G. Carter. *Coastal Dunes: Form and Process.* New York: Wiley and Sons, 1990. A technical book on the formation and characteristics of coastal dunes.

NWS (National Weather Service). *Hurricane Andrew: South Florida and Louisiana, August 23–26, 1992.* Silver Spring, Md.: U.S. Department of Commerce, National Oceanic and Atmospheric Administration, Natural Disaster Survey Report, 131 pages, Appendices A–G, and an Afterword, 1993. This book discusses the damages in Florida and Louisiana from Hurricane Andrew in 1992.

Pielke, R. A. Jr., and R. A. Pielke Sr. *Hurricanes, Their Nature and Impacts on Society.* New York: John Wiley & Sons, Ltd. 1998. This book discusses hurricane damage and the social impacts that they have on communities and society as a whole.

Pilkey, O. H., and W. J. Neal. "Coastal Geologic Hazards." In *The Geology of North America*, edited by R. E. Sheridan, and J. A. Grow, Volume 1–2, The Atlantic Continental Margin, U.S. Geological Society of America, 1988. This is a comprehensive survey and review of coastal hazards on the eastern coast of North America.

Salvador, A., ed. *The Gulf of Mexico Basin, Geology of North America v. J.* Boulder, Colo.: Geological Society of America, 1991. This reference discusses the detailed geologic evolution of the Gulf of Mexico basin, including the Mississippi Delta.

Schuck-Kolben, R. Erik. *Storm-tide Elevations Produced by Hurricane Hugo along the South Carolina coast, September 21–22, 1989.* Reston, Va.: U.S. Geological Survey Open-File Report OF 90-0386, prepared in cooperation with the Federal Emergency Management Agency, 31 sheets, 1990. These maps and report show the exceptionally high storm surge associated with the approach of Hurricane Hugo to the coast of South Carolina in 1989.

Shinkle, K. D., and R. K. Dokka. *Rates of Vertical Displacement at Benchmarks in the Lower Mississippi Valley and the Northern Gulf Coast.* Washington, D.C.: NOAA Technical Report NOS/NGS 50, 2004. This important report evaluates the subsidence of the Mississippi Delta, and shows that the rates are greater than previously appreciated.

Simpson, R. H., and H. Riehl. *The Hurricane and its Impact.* Baton Rouge: Louisiana State University Press, 1981. This book, written for a general audience, discusses the formation of hurricanes and how they affect coastal areas.

Stringer-Robinson, G. *Time and Tide on Folly Beach, South Carolina (a history).* Folly Beach, S.C.: Gretchen Stringer-Robinson, 1989. A well-written history of the barrier island (Folly Beach) off South Carolina.

USACOE (U.S. Army Corps of Engineers). *Shore Protection Manual.* Washington, D.C.: U.S. Government Printing Office; stock no. 008-022-00218-9, three volumes, 1984. This book outlines a strategy to protect certain areas along beaches and shorelines.

Williams, S. J., K. Dodd, and K. K. Gohn. *Coasts in Crisis.* Reston, Va.: U.S. Geological Survey Circular 1075, 1990. This book discusses how beach environments are threatened by overuse, construction, damming of rivers, and changing sea levels.

JOURNAL ARTICLES

Clayton, T. D. "Beach Replenishment Activities on U.S. Continental Pacific Coast." *Journal of Coastal Research* 7, no. 4 (1991): 1,195–1,210. This report discusses the different efforts to keep sand on beaches in coastal California, Oregon, and Washington.

Coch, N. K., and M. P. Wolff. "Effects of Hurricane Hugo Storm Surge in Coastal South Carolina" in C. W. Finkl, and O. H. Pilkey, eds., Impacts of Hurricane Hugo: September 10–22, 1989. *Journal of Coastal Research Special Issue* 8 (1991): 201–228. A discussion of the damage from the catastrophic storm surge from Hurricane Hugo in South Carolina.

Davis, Robert E., and Robert Dolan. "Nor'easters." *American Scientist* 81 (1993): 428–439.

Dixon, K. and O. H. Pilkey. "Summary of Beach Replenishment on the U.S. Gulf of Mexico Shoreline." *Journal of Coastal Research* 7, no. 1 (1991): 249–256. This report discusses the different efforts to keep sand on beaches along the Gulf of Mexico.

Dolan, R., P. J. Godfrey, and W. E. Odum. "Man's Impact on the Barrier Islands of North Carolina." *American Scientist* 61 (1973): 152–162. A discussion of how development has affected the barrier beaches of North Carolina.

Dolan, Robert, and Robert E. Davis. "An Intensity Scale for Atlantic Coast Northeast Storms." *Journal of Coastal Research* 8, no. 4 (1992): 840–853. This report discusses the commonly used Saffir-Simpson scale used to measure hurricane intensity.

Godfrey, P.J. "Barrier Beaches of the East Coast." *Oceanus,* 19, no. 5 (1976): 27–40. This report presents a summary of the characteristics of barrier beaches and islands along the eastern seaboard of the United States, 1976.

Horton, T. "Hanging in the Balance—Chesapeake Bay." *National Geographic,* 183, no. 6, (1993): 2–35. This general article describes the fragile estuary ecosystem of Chesapeake Bay.

Kraus, Nicholas C., and O. H. Pilkey, "The Effects of Seawalls on the Beach." *Journal of Coastal Research,* Special Issue no. 4 (1988). This article describes how seawalls focus energy downward and increase beach erosion.

Penland, S., H. H. Roberts, S. J. Williams, D. R. Sallenger, D. R. Cahoon, D. W. Davis, and C. G. Groat. "Coastal Land Loss in Louisiana." *Transactions Gulf Coast Association of Geological Societies* XL (1990): 685–699.

Pilkey, Orrin H.. "Coastal Erosion." *Episodes* 14 no. 1 (1991): 46–51. This short article presents evidence for rapid erosion along many beaches and sea cliffs in the United States.

Sever, M. "Confusion Over Sinking Coasts in the Gulf." *Geotimes* (August 2005): 10–12. This article present a review of the different lines of evidence used to determine the subsidence rates of the coast along the Gulf of Mexico.

Simpson, R. H. "The Hurricane Disaster Potential Scale." *Weatherwise XXVII*: 169 (1974): 186. This article presents the definition of the currently used Saffir-Simpson scale of hurricane intensity.

Waltham, T. "The Flooding of New Orleans." *Geology Today* 21, no. 6 (2005): 225–231. This article presents a readable summary of the main flooding events from Hurricane Katrina in New Orleans.

INTERNET RESOURCES

In the past few years, numerous Web sites with information about coastal hazards, hurricanes, and storms have appeared. Most of these Web sites are free, and include historical information about specific hazards and disasters, real-time monitoring of active hurricanes around the world, and educational material. The sites listed below have interesting information, statistics, and graphics about these hazards. This book may serve as a useful companion while surfing through the information on the Internet when encountering unfamiliar phrases, terms, or concepts that are not fully explained on the Web site. The following list of Web sites is recommended to help enrich the content of this book and make your exploration of coastal processes, hurricanes, and subsidence more enjoyable. In addition, any hurricanes or coastal disasters that occur after this book goes to press will be discussed on these Web sites, so checking the Web sites listed here can help you keep this book up to date. From these Web sites you will also be able to link to a large variety of hazard-related sites. Every effort has been made to ensure the accuracy of the information provided for these Web sites. However, due to the dynamic nature of the Internet, changes might occur, and any inconvenience is regretted.

Federal Emergency Management Agency. Available online. URL: http://www.fema.gov. Accessed May 23, 2007. FEMA is the nation's premier agency that deals with emergency management and preparation, and issues warnings and evacuation orders when disasters appear imminent. FEMA maintains a Web site that is updated at least daily, includes information of hurricanes, floods, fires, national flood insurance, and information on disaster prevention, preparation, emergency management. It is divided into national and regional sites and also contains information on costs of disasters, maps, and directions on how to do business with FEMA.

National Aeronautic and Space Administration. Available online. URL: http://earthobservatory.nasa.gov/NaturalHazards/. Accessed May 23, 2007. This is NASA's Web site on natural hazards: Earth scientists around the world use NASA satellite imagery to better understand the causes and effects of natural hazards. This site posts many public domain images to help people visualize where and when natural hazards occur, and to help mitigate their effects. All images in this section are freely available to the public for reuse or republication.

National Oceanographic and Atmospheric Administration, Hazards research. Available online. URL: http://ngdc.noaa.gov/seg/hazard/tsu.html Accessed March 28, 2007. This is a Web site about hazards, including coastal hazards. NOAA conducts research and gathers data about the global oceans, atmosphere, space and the Sun, and applies this knowledge to science and service that touch lives of all Americans. NOAA's mission is to describe and predict changes in Earth's environment, and conserve and wisely manage the nation's coastal and marine resources. NOAA's strategy consists of seven interrelated strategic goals for environmental assessment, prediction and stewardship. These include (1) advance short-term warnings and forecast services, (2) implement season to interannual climate forecasts, (3) assess and predict decadal to centennial change, (4) promote safe navigation, (5) build sustainable fisheries, (6) recover protected species, and (7) sustain healthy coastal ecosystems. NOAA runs a Web site that includes links to current satellite images of weather hazards, issues warnings of current coastal hazards and disasters, and has an extensive historical and educational service.

Natural Hazards Observer. Available online URL: http://www.colorado. edu/hazards/o/. Accessed May 23, 2007. This Web site is the online version of the periodical, *The Natural Hazards Observer. The Natural Hazards Observer* is the bimonthly periodical of the Natural Hazards Center. It covers current disaster issues; new international, national, and local disaster management, mitigation, and education programs; hazards research; political and policy developments; new information sources and Web sites; upcoming conferences; and recent publications. Distributed to over 15,000 subscribers in the United States and abroad via printed copies their Web site, the *Observer* focuses on news regarding human adaptation and response to natural hazards and other catastrophic events and provides a forum for concerned individuals to express opinions and generate new ideas through invited personal articles.

U.S. Army Corps of Engineers. Available online. URL: http://www.erdc. usace.army.mil/ http://www.usace.army.mil/public.html#REstate. The U.S. Army Corps of Engineers has an emergency response unit, set for responding to environmental, coastal, and other disasters. The Headquaters Office, http://www.usace.army.mil/where.html#Headquarters, is a good place to start a search for any specific problem.

United States Geological Survey, hazards research. Available online. URL: http://www.usgs.gov/themes/hazard.html. Accessed May 23, 2007. This Web site has descriptions of geological hazards, with pages on coastal hazards. In the United States each year, natural hazards cause hundreds of deaths and cost tens of billions of dollars in disaster aid, disruption of commerce, and destruction of homes and critical infrastructure. This series of web pages was designed to educate citizens, emergency managers, and lawmakers on seven natural hazards facing the nation—earthquakes, floods, hurricanes, landslides, tsunamis, volcanoes, and wildfires—and show how USGS science helps mitigate disasters and build resilient communities.

Index

Note: Page numbers in *italic* refer to illustrations, *m* indicates a map, *t* indicates a table.